Metaphysical Anatomy

EVETTE ROSE

Volume 2

Version 2.4

EVETTE ROSE

... there is more

There is a discussion forum dedicated to Metaphysical Anatomy. The site includes updates with new medical conditions upon request. New discoveries and new articles related to important and interesting topics will be shared. Evette will also answer questions that you might have. The forum has also been developed with the intention for subscribers to brainstorm new ideas, approaches and research that can help and support each other as well as people who are new to the metaphysical anatomy topic. You will also receive powerful transformational meditations designed and recorded by Evette Rose. In order to receive the full benefits of membership please visit www.evetterose.com for more information.

ISBN-13: 978-1492297925
ISBN-10: 1492297925

METAPHYSICAL ANATOMY VOLUME 2

Disclaimer

All information obtained from Evette Rose or anything written or said by her, is to be taken solely as advisory in nature. Evette Rose and Inner Beauty States will not be held personally, legally, or financially liable for any action taken based upon their advice. Evette Rose is not a psychologist or medical professional and is unable to diagnose, prescribe, treat, or cure any ailment. Anyone using the information in this book acknowledges that they have read and understand the details of this disclaimer. Evette can discuss the metaphysical explanations for psychological disorders but are unable to diagnose, prescribe, treat, or claim to cure any illnesses that require medical or psychiatric attention. The principles taught in Inner Beauty States, Metaphysical Anatomy and discussed Key Points are guidelines and suggestions for the facilitator to support their client through personal development sessions. By utilizing and using this book, the participant acknowledges that he/she assumes full responsibility for the knowledge gained herein and its application. Material in this book is not intended to replace the advice of a competent healthcare practitioner. The reader takes full responsibility for the way they utilize and exercise the information in this book.

Legal

All recordings and publications obtained from Evette Rose and Inner Beauty States, or this book remain the intellectual property of the aforementioned and must not be used or reprinted in any way without the written permission of Evette Rose. Any unauthorized commercial use of Evette Rose's name, photograph, images, or written material is strictly prohibited and is in direct violation of rights.

.

Also by Evette Rose

Finding Your Own Voice

2ⁿᵈ Edition

Finding Your Own Voice

Your past can control who you are, until you find your own voice.

www.EvetteRose.com

Also by Evette Rose
Metaphysical Anatomy
Volume 1

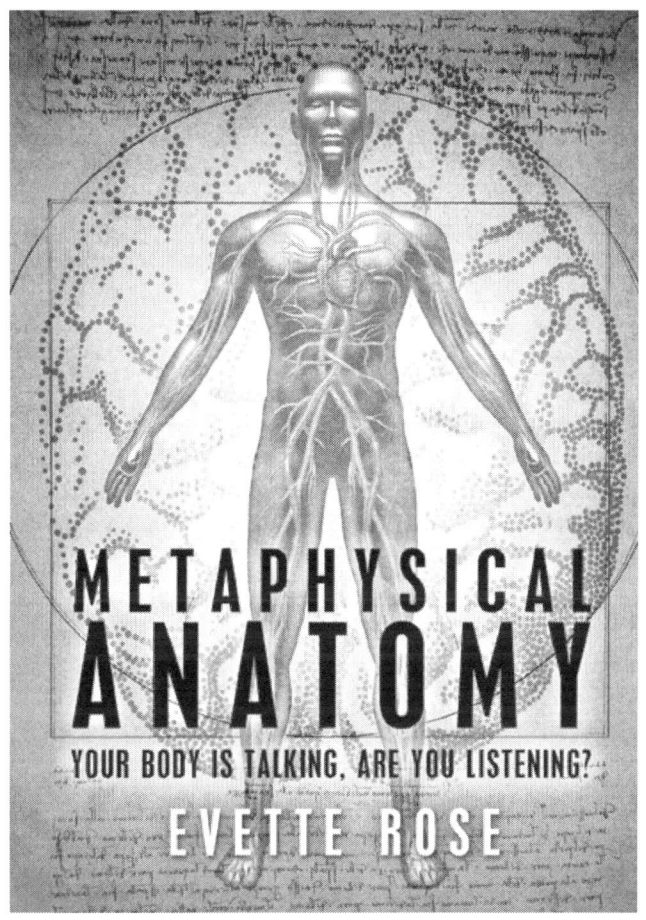

Your Body is Talking, are You Listening?

Volume 1, this version of Metaphysical Anatomy is more comprehensive and in-depth for those who are serious about their personal development journey! This volume is so much more than just illnesses from A – Z. Metaphysical Anatomy Volume 1 also includes step-by-step guide for identifying the origin of the disease process, whether it be in your ancestry, conception, womb, birth or childhood. It also guides alternative practitioners in effective ways to sharpen their practicing skills. This book is equally valuable for experienced alternative healing practitioners, psychotherapists, hypnotherapists, personal development coaches and those interested in self-healing.

ACKNOWLEDGMENTS

Thank you to each and every client or student that I have met for your insight, support and willingness to share your life stories. I would not have been able to write this book without you!

Thank you Elizabeth Baker for your support with the English editing process, it was a pleasure to work with you!

With Love,

Evette Rose

TABLE OF CONTENTS

Introduction

Congratulations on taking the first step to understanding the body and its messages. Metaphysical Anatomy Volume 2 was an introduction to its bigger brother, Metaphysical Anatomy Volume 1. The focus of the book is to help alternative practitioners sharpen their skills and for those interested in self-healing to understand the language of their body on a deeper and more meaning level. Here I share short but powerful key emotional patterns and trauma that relates to certain medical conditions. In Metaphysical Anatomy Volume 1, I take the information shared in this book to a new and much deeper level. In Volume 1 I also share key points that gives guidance to the reader where and how certain medical may start. Keep an open mind and the possibilities will be endless while you explore the content in this fantastic reference guide!

Evette Rose is also founder of Inner Beauty States. For more information about Metaphysical Anatomy Volume 1, please visit www.EvetteRose.com.

Recovering Your Natural Emotional States Permanently

Let's start by defining what a state is. A state is a present condition or consciousness of a person at any given time. This state can positive or negative depending on the person's circumstances which could either have a negative or positive effect on them.

We are always trying to access positive states in life by engaging in activities such as drinking or participating in sports activities (running for example). Everybody knows unconsciously that there is a memory of these positive states that they sometimes feel momentarily. We lose these states during our developmental events (e.g. trauma) where trauma blocks a person from experiencing certain states. As a result, we only experience momentary glimpses of these states. These states often come to the surface involuntarily or when we engage in certain activities. When these states are temporarily recovered while we engage in certain activities such as running for example, we associate this activity with the positive state that we experience. We keep repeating these activities with the intention of continually accessing these states. However, the states that we achieve and feel are only temporary, as any trauma that is blocking them, has not been resolved.

How can you maintain these states that you only seem to catch glimpses of? The answer is simple. You would need to resolve specific traumas that took place at particular developmental events in order to recover your natural states.

Some examples of different states that we are born with are: Freedom State, Inner Balance State, Gratitude State and the Here and Now State. I am just giving these emotional states names so that we have specific emotional states to refer to during this introduction. Most people cannot access their natural emotional states as their states were suppressed by trauma. The trauma that blocks these states often takes place during a person's conception, birth and childhood stages. Once certain trauma points have been released, our natural emotional states are automatically restored and we can enjoy our natural states on a permanent basis. Once trauma that blocks our states has been resolved, the state that is recovered is lasting. The specific points that were unblocked in your biology stay cleared and your state is always active.

These states help you to manage your emotions and greatly improve your quality of life. Your emotional intelligence and awareness are heightened and you are not driven and controlled by the intense emotions that were once held in place by specific traumas. When your natural states are recovered, you can then manage your overall emotional state better than the average person who has not recovered their natural states. When your emotions are activated, you can blindly do things that you might regret later on. The states work to help you control these impulsive urges and bring you back to a more grounded frame of mind. You are able to make better decisions with more objectivity, clarity and discernment. These are just some of the many benefits you will get from recovering your natural states.

When we experience trauma, it greatly affects the way we see the world. Whether this trauma occurred before or during conception / birth, it will have an affect. Decisions, reactions and interactions between others and us are influenced by trauma. When trauma is healed, you experience more than just relief from stress. It changes how you experience your life, interact with others and most important of all, it changes and greatly improves the way you see yourself and the world. Your judgment towards life and people changes, as it is not affected by trauma. Your perception is not controlled by past trauma. You are able to start seeing and observing people more clearly, with more, understanding and compassion. You are also less emotionally activated as old trauma has been lifted and healed. This means that you do not have as much trauma that can be activated in your daily life. It truly takes the definition of emotional freedom to a new level!

Our natural states are calm; there is no trauma associated with our natural states. This means that when we experience The Gratitude State for example, you feel a gentle and calm state of gratitude towards yourself, others and your environment. States are by their very nature, gentle; they are not heightened emotions. When you experience a state, you feel calm and peaceful along with the description (symptoms) of the state that was recovered. Our natural states are calm and peaceful. There should be no charge, such as positive or negative. Even heightened positive states such as nervous laughter or even excitement can and will still drain your energy and even though you associate positive experiences with these emotional reactions doesn't mean that they are always necessarily good for us. Anything that can potentially drain the body energetically is considered trauma (yes that includes positive trauma). Positive trauma is trauma and depletes you either way. Our natural states are consistent and gentle and do not cause any stress to the body. Our natural states are there to keep us calm, in harmony and coherent within ourselves and within our environment.

Natural States that are now being recovered

Freedom State

This state will enable you to reach a more peaceful mental state. There will be less clutter in your mind. This state will also create a desire to change things around in your life and to find a direction that suits your needs and future goals. Summarized in short, if something needs to give in your life then this state will bring it about quicker and give you the drive to move forward. You will reinvent your life in a way that will give you the freedom that you need and desire in order to reach your highest potential. You will notice gentle effects and results of the Freedom State for four months after process.

An important observation that we made was that people needed to let go of certain habits, patterns and relationships that no longer serve them. This state will put the wheel of change in motion and push you to make the necessary changes. You will start to recognize and feel that which no longer serves your purpose, especially if you are not doing what you feel you are meant to do or if you are not with the right partner, for example.

The Freedom State will require you to make changes in your life. For this reason, you might not feel the results straight away. You feel suddenly that you are free and feeling free from cultural expectations, projections of others and stigmas. Past activities that were driven and motivated by trauma start to dissolve. You will find that after recovering this state, it will be more challenging for others to manipulate you as well.

Gratitude State

Blocks that hindered your ability to be fully present in your life will be lifted and cleared when this state is recovered. You will be more receptive to your environment, feel your emotions and you will be more open to becoming aware of blessings that you surrounded by in life. Your perception and the way you perceive your reality is not blocked and filtered by trauma. You are able to see and experience positive aspects to all situations and interactions with people. This state also raises your relationship with yourself to a new and profound level, as you will find that you feel more appreciative of yourself and what you have achieved in your life. You will feel a great sense of gratitude toward yourself and others. This state also makes it easier to forgive and forget, as you are able to see the teaching and learning in each situation, instead of staring yourself blind with resentment and blame. It enables you to see 'the other side' of the story when caught up in disputes, as well. You will find that you are more centered and calm in the face of adversity, as it will be easier for you to see and hear another person's point of view. You experience conflict in a calmer fashion. This state is also wonderful for people who experienced abuse, as it helps the person to focus more on the good aspects of their life rather than resenting their circumstances. They are able to see the blessings in their current life, thereby greatly improving their quality of life!

Being Here and Now

You feel that you become one with the world; there is a sense of oneness and you no longer have that sense of 'separation.' Your inner world feels connected to the outside world; you feel more connected to nature and you will also find that you have a deeper and more meaningful connection with people who also have this state. It takes the concept of being present to a new level! Your 3-D vision becomes deeper and clearer, your surroundings become full of life. You start to feel connected to the people and things that you once took for granted. Your peripheral vision widens and you are able to keep your focus for longer and you are more present with people in your environment. You feel serene, blissful, peaceful and grounded. You will feel that all is well. This state is great for children, as it helps to keep them more present and stabilizes them to a great extent.

Inner Balance

The name says it all. You will discover that you find your balance and coherent state much quicker after an argument or trauma. It gives you peace of mind and helps you to feel more comfortable within yourself. You don't always feel so activated by your environment and there is a deeper sense of calmness and peace in your life.

More Personal Development Packages

Disconnection Process

The Disconnect Process will assist you in letting go of people that no longer serve you. It will also help you to let go of unhealthy attachments that you have with people that are not for your highest and best. This process releases a great deal of emotional stress and the neediness you may feel toward the person you would like to disconnect from; they will no longer have free rent in your mind.

Letting Go Package - Healing from Divorce or Break-up

This package is designed to assist those who would like to move on in their lives from trauma experienced as a result of divorce or separation. It will bring about the forgiveness stage much quicker. You'll be relieved from feeling afraid of moving forward with your life. Trauma related to isolation, separation, rejection and a sense of failure would also be addressed and resolved, as well. The package includes The Disconnect Process, as this process perfectly rounds off the Healing from Divorce or Break-up Process. Feelings of attachment and neediness toward someone that you need to let go of in your life will be resolved.

Inner Goddess State

This process will resolve trauma related to your sexuality, personal boundaries, being and feeling attractive. You will recover your natural beauty state and regain confidence in your feminine qualities. You will feel equal to others and have more confidence in yourself and your appearance.

More packages are currently being designed, please visit http://evetterose.com/inner-beauty-states/ the latest states and packages updates.

The below topics are discussed in Volume 1

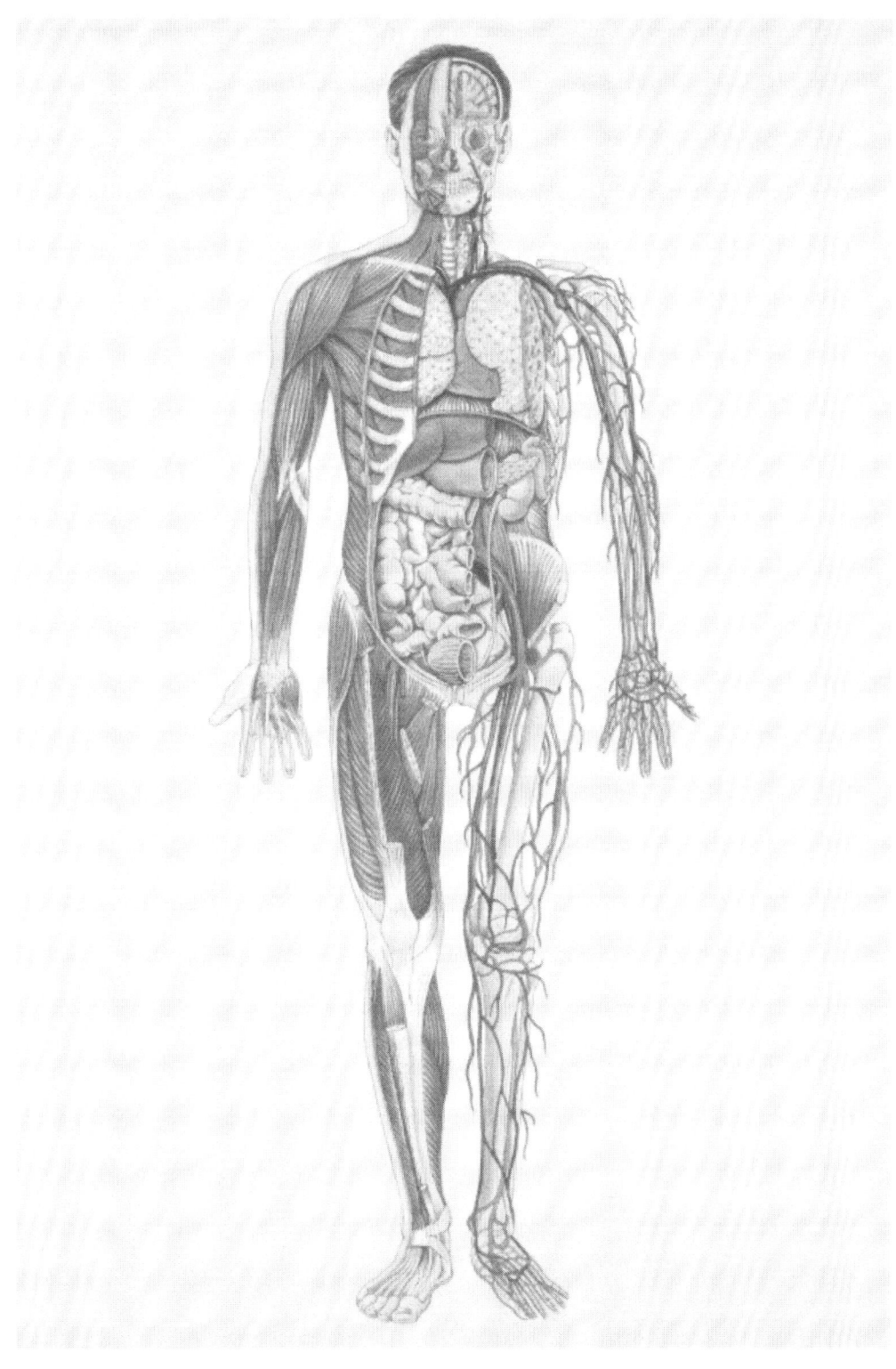

Quick Reference Guide

Body Part	Possible Key Emotions
Age spots	Skin trauma stemming from ancestry line due to sun exposure. Feeling resentful toward circumstances. Frustration and irritation that has grown out of control.
Ankles	Flexibility related to the future, control issues, stubbornness and conflict with mother.
Anus	Refusal to let go of bad and sabotaging patterns that are still serving you. Holding onto toxic and unhealthy love and relationships.
Arteries	One's ability to give to others and support (fear of giving too much of yourself, fear of being depleted or taken advantage of).
Arms	Fear of being powerful and reclaiming your own personal power and identity.
Back	Support, structure, responsibility, stability.
Middle Back	Feeling responsible for others, blurred line between what is your issue and what is not. Humiliation, embarrassment; feeling dominated and controlled.
Lower Back	Financial responsibilities, others needs, burdens; feeling under pressure.
Bacteria	Guilt and regret, self-punishment, sabotage.
Bladder	Feeling pissed off with people in authority. Feeling helpless and disempowered to change your circumstances.
Uthera	Drawing power from your feelings of resentment, don't want to let go of toxic relationships. Feel suppressed and resentful leading to hardening of the attitude. Feel attacked by loved ones.
Blood	How you feel about your appearance, how you communicate your needs, life force. How protected you feel from the world.
Bones	Needing to be strong, feeling supported, loyalty of others toward you.
Bones broken	Support has been pulled out from under you. Losing control of your life. Fear of change. Sabotaging personal progress. Needing to break away from old habits and take more time to make decisions.

Body Part	Possible Key Emotions
Brain	Control issues, what you see and feel are not coherent, resulting in conflict. Feeling unable to control what your brain senses, your connection to your environment is traumatic.
Breasts	Nurture, love, mother love, giving and receiving nurturing, abuse trauma, relationship with close family members.
Bunions	Feeling vulnerable and exposed in your quest to move away from family values. Stubbornness, "I will show you." Pushing too hard—can only have fun when working really hard.
Cheeks	Insecurities. Feel intimidated by authority and confrontation.
Chest	Feel pushed away by a mother and also pushing people away. Negative association with love.
Chin	Worthiness, anger related to words you cannot express. Feel betrayed yet unable to say anything about it. Your truth is not believed.
Ear	What don't you want to hear, need to block out; who or what? Fear of confrontation. Feel disempowered by influential people.
Elbow	Poor personal boundaries. Need to push people away. Hardening of the attitude. Indecisiveness, "Should I or shouldn't I?" Lack of passion related to what you do in life. Elbow problems are related to feeling very indecisive. Not knowing whether to leave or continue a project, job or relationship. Feeling obligated to see things through however, even though there is no benefit for you.
Eyebrows	Need to be different than others. Don't feel unique and good enough as you are. Lack of acknowledgement and praise.
Eyes	Seeing truth, resistance to not seeing your environment, too much responsibility, wanting to hide. Related to birth trauma.
Fat	Protection. Being unattractive = feeling safe. Trauma related to scarcity such as food, love and protection. Trauma related to being a threat to someone. Love and relationships = toxicity.
Feet	Stepping forward, control, direction, stubbornness, feel controlled and out of control, resistance to change, fear of moving away from family and family values.
Fingers	Feel unsure where you fit in, needing to establish your identity, to be validated, do not feel supported when doing things. Holding back secrets, direction in life, passion. See the Fingers section.
Forehead	Feel conflicted and angry due to current circumstances and people in your immediate environment. Feel like losing control.

Body Part	Possible Key Emotions
Fungus	Resentment related to a mother / feminine figure. Abandonment trauma.
Glands	Feeling unable to express boundaries. Holding back anger as a result of recent circumstances. Represents how you feel about your situation.
Gums	Feeling attacked, unsupported when making decisions. Feel unable to change / break away from unhealthy circumstances. Anger is your best defense.
Hair	How you feel about yourself. Feeling unprotected. Need to get away / escape circumstances or someone. Feel controlled and threatened. Disassociated from feelings.
Hands	Blocks around receiving, giving, delegating without guilt, understanding how you feel when you are working (such as in the workplace).
Head	Connection to self, life purpose, identity, feeling controlled.
Heart	Giving and receiving of love and nurturing. The Left side ventricle is related to receiving. The Right side ventricle is related to giving. Also related to one's territory and competitiveness.
Hip	Balance and moving forward, being flexible, relationship problems, sexuality, confidence in personal relationships.
Infection	Resentment and anger grown out of control. Disgusted with self, feeling shame and suppressing feelings of panic.
Intestines	Store old abuse, store resentment, anger, vengeance, injustice and betrayal within close relationships.
Jaw	How one expresses oneself to parents—what is the conflict?
Kidney	Resentment, anger, not letting go, toxic relationships.
Knees	Moving forward, making big changes, fear of what others might think if you follow your own beliefs and values. Fear of stepping into influential roles; feel pushed down and controlled by a feminine figure.
Cut on Knee	Your goals and needs are attacked, criticized and unsupported by influential people.
Lips	Feeling insecure and overly aware of how others view you. Fear and tension related to what you need to say. You don't trust your own judgment.
Liver	Regret, resentment, guilt because of what one cannot change. Anger related to feeling suppressed, loss of identity.

Body Part	Possible Key Emotions
Lungs	Grief, depression, sorrow, lack of joy, feeling smothered, suppressed and controlled by those you rely on for love.
Lymph nodes	Knowing what is good / bad for oneself. Self-sabotaging health and happiness. Stuck in unhealthy / undesirable circumstances and feeling helpless to change it. Feeling under attack.
Muscles	How one feels about oneself, stubbornness, having to be right, holding on to guilt.
Myelin Sheath	Trauma related to communication. Blocking what you see and sense in your environment. Self-sabotage of personal progress. Love in your life feels toxic, stressful and invasive.
Nails	Feeling unprotected, controlled and manipulated by authority.
Neck	Rigidity, not able to make decisions, resisting your environment. Feel vulnerable and out of your depth within circumstances and relationships. Not allowed to be with someone else.
Nerves	Communication trauma. Ability to communicate is being controlled and manipulated by authority.
Nose (see Sinus)	Personal power, how strong do you feel when outside of your comfort zone? Trauma related to intuition and psychic abilities. Your character feels under attack.
Parasites	Boundary issues, invasion, not feeling worthy of saying "no."
Pelvis	Ancestral trauma related to sexual abuse, feeling unimportant, cannot stand your ground, feel powerless.
Rashes	Built-up trauma related to fear of confrontation, verbal or physical abuse. Take things too personally.
Ribs	Feel ignored by family, unable to protect what matters to me.
Shoulders	Carrying responsibility (Financial / Family) / guilt about having fun
Sinus / Blocked nose	Trauma related to intuition and psychic abilities. Feel offended and invaded by environment. Feel rejected and abandoned. Disconnected from feeling joy.
Skin	Irritation, sensitivity to specific issues / people, lack of protection, poor personal boundaries, holding on to anger and resentment, feeling vulnerable.
Spine	Structure, direction in life, burdens, financial responsibility, sexuality, reproducing, breadwinner.
Swelling	Boundary failures resulted in anger and feeling helpless. You are not expressing clear boundaries.

Body Part	Possible Key Emotions
Teeth	How supported and protected you felt during your childhood and womb stages.
Tendon	There is urgency to what you want to do, feel pressured; everyone is watching my every move.
Tongue	You are not sharing your opinion. Feel silenced by authority.
Veins	Feels blocked around receiving love and support. Receiving may have equaled feeling obligated, controlled. Love = abuse / lack.
Virus	Worthiness, disappointment, self-punishment, poor personal boundaries, having to fight for respect and understanding.
Warts	Feeling resentful toward influential people for projecting too much responsibility onto you. People in your life feel energetically parasitic. Feelings of resentment have grown out of control.
Wrists	Feel that you are the buffer between two people, feeling caught in the middle of something. Fear of failure.

Abasia

See Athetosis, Chorea, Meniere's Disease, Paralysis, Tic, Tremor

Emotions

Choreic abasia: is an abnormal involuntary movement of the legs. You should explore patterns such as suppressed fear and shock. Have you been pushed into doing something that you didn't want to do, or were not emotionally and mentally ready for? Explore your parent's history related to feeling forced to do things against their will. This could include being sent to boarding school or events that are more traumatic that were outside of their control. You may feel stuck in a fight or flight instinct conflicting with a dominating freeze instinct.

Discussed in Volume 1: Paralytic abasia, Spastic abasia and Trembling abasia.

Abortion

See Attack, Birth, Miscarriage, Eclampsia, Post-Traumatic Stress Disorder, Pregnancy, Toxins, Uterus Problems

Emotions

There could be several reasons why a mother would abort a pregnancy. Sexual assault, life threatening conditions or defects in the developing fetus could all be reasons for the abortion. Regardless of why the abortion took place, it is a traumatic and heart wrenching situation for someone to experience. Many women suffer from depression, PTSD, guilt and shame after an abortion. These symptoms may be triggered by the abortion but in fact, the abortion may just be the final tipping point in a pattern of pre-existing trauma.

Discussed in Volume 1: For mother aborting pregnancy, Survivor of an attempted abortion, Child born to woman who had previous abortion.

Abscess

See Inflammation / Infection, Parasites

Emotions

You have been suppressing anger, rage and resentment for long periods of time. The suppression has now begun to surface on a physical level. Children often develop this condition when they feel that influential people are suppressing them. You may not feel validated by someone whose opinion is valued. Repetitive and unresolved quarrels/confrontations in the environment seem to be affecting you and lead to feelings of being overwhelmed. Conversations in the mind seem to keep you mentally occupied, taking the focus away from how you really feel in the heart mind. The idea of letting go of anger and circumstances that are unhealthy seems to be a challenge. Familiar feelings such as anger, resentment and trauma feel more empowering than gentler feelings such as happiness. Personal relationships seem to have a love-hate pattern, whether it is with a partner, friend, co-worker or family member. You have now reached a point where you've had enough. As a result of internal conflict, you are physically drained. Suppressed anger has left an emotional scar, which serves as a reminder that it is time to resolve problems before they grow out of control.

Abundance discussed in Volume 1.

Accidents

See Back Problems, Bone Problems, Pain, Paralyzed

Emotions

Trauma related to an accident (or car accident) in your past is still being expressed and triggered in your day-to-day life. You feel out of control while the freeze instinct is activated during an accident. The freeze instinct locks in the trauma (including the emotions, physical pain and shock felt) at the time of the accident. Emotions, shock and trauma are locked into the body mind at the same time. In the future, when you find yourself in a similar emotional or physical situation, you feel the same emotions and trigger the unresolved secondary trauma that stemmed from the initial accident. At this point, you may be experiencing the old trauma that was triggered, secondary trauma related to the accident and new trauma! What complicates matters is that you need to address the origin of the trauma, not these symptoms.

Achilles Tendon Rupture

See Muscle Problems, Rupture, Plantar Fasciitis, Tendon Problems

Emotions

Once you begin a project or have a goal in mind, you are determined to get it done. You do not like changes and amendments to what you have started and created in life. Because of past regrets and circumstances you were unable to control, you often feel angry and resentful. You may feel like you were manipulated and controlled by influential people who used fear and shame to put you in your place. Now you may feel unsure of how to create your own future with confidence. You are afraid of failing without the support and guidance of influential people. You feel resentful because you gave your power away and now you want it back. Only now, you feel like you have to ask for your power—you can't just reach for it. Sabotaging your own goals and future is the safest option, as then there can be no surprises. You are determined and stubborn, often putting a great deal of pressure on yourself to avoid making a mistake or failing. In the past, when you received support it was in the form of pressure and manipulation. You now use that same method to motivate yourself—you think that success = pressure. You work hard and become even more stubborn, creating a cycle where stubbornness = power and endurance.

Acid Reflux

See Nausea, Reflux, Rumination Syndrome

Emotions

The circumstances you are currently dealing with are emotionally and mentally unhealthy for you—you literally cannot stomach them! You have a fear of confronting people who challenge you and as a result, you have set poor personal boundaries, which get in the way of expressing yourself clearly. You often find that people walk all over you, leaving you frustrated and resentful. You are filled with doubt and question your ability to successfully change difficult circumstances that no longer work. You are afraid of changing anything in you life, including any patterns, habits and survival instincts that still serve you. Your fear of being alone has allowed you to remain in unhealthy relationships, rather than face being on your own. Having company around is very important, making you feel safe and comforted. This could be the result of a physically or mentally abusive childhood, whether it took place at home / school / after care. You feel challenged and judged by dominant figures in your life to the point where you feel unsafe in being yourself. You often communicate in intense and passionate ways, making a point in a conversation with a lasting impact makes you feel heard and respected. Paranoia and a need to control often dominate your head mind. You have been suppressing strong emotions, as you have been bullied whenever you attempt to step into your power.

Acne

See Bacteria, Boils

Emotions

You may be painfully shy and unsure of where you stand in the world. You have reached a point where you've had enough of feeling stuck, without direction. At this point, your frustration and anger have reached a boiling point, almost simmering under the skin. You have come to resent how easy it seems for others to fit into social groups while you feel less than worthy. You have trouble believing in your own abilities to be successful or independent and see other's success as a reminder of what you may never achieve.

Adults with acne

Similar issues as mentioned above are currently taking place in your life. There is trauma that took place during the teenage years that hasn't been resolved.

Acoustic Neuroma

See Cancer, Nerves, Trigeminal Neuralgia, Tumors

Emotions

Invasive family members have challenged your right to have privacy since childhood, making it difficult to discern appropriate boundaries and interactions. A controlling parent/influential authority figure twisted your truth. The parent / guardian didn't respect your emotions, privacy or feelings and you lacked sufficient support and respect from family members. You were made to feel ashamed for expressing boundaries. Deep down you are painfully shy and are very conscious of how the world perceives you. Letting people into your life can be experienced as an invasion, so isolation feels comforting and peaceful. Expressing the truth is often challenging. In the past, your truth was often twisted into information that was considered unimportant. Now you doubt your own judgment and the power to make decisions. Your parents communicated in such a way that was not entirely clear, leaving you confused about expectations. Misunderstanding often led to resistance and rebellion on your part. By suppressing your emotions, you were able to avoid punishment—it was your saving grace.

Acute Interstitial Pneumonitis

See Asbestos, Lung Problems, Pneumonia

Emotions

You feel attacked (verbally or physically) by loved ones, hurt by those who should provide protection, love and nurturing. Emotional and physical needs have been met by inconsistent reactions of influential people. As a result, you feel intimidated by the behavior of loved ones and the way they express "love." You may feel scattered and confused, with no clear direction to head in with your goals. A great deal of grief is being suppressed, while you long for others that resonate with you. Your ability to suppress your feelings and your past is beginning to fail and you feel suffocated by circumstances that have grown out of control. This impossible situation is taking a toll and throwing in the towel is starting to look like the only available option. You feel that the odds are against you and no amount of support can change that.

Acute Lymphoblastic Leukemia

See Anemia, Blood Problems, Leukemia

Emotions

You may have a great need to protect yourself from harsh conditions, such as abusive family members and challenging circumstances. You may also feel a need to protect someone who is close to you, by making it a priority to comfort and resolve his or her trauma and pain. This kind of behavior often stems from a need to be protected from harsh people or circumstances. You feel attacked by those who should have loved you—your need for love was met by abuse and hostility.

Addictions

See Anxiety, Depression, Caesarean, Hyperventilation, Hysteria, Nervous Breakdown, Post-Traumatic Stress Disorder PTSD, Tremor

General remarks: Your mother may have been abused while she was pregnant with you. She may have lived in fear of her partner or her environment which resulted in her body being stuck in a fight or flight mode. The fetus may have developed in a stressful environment, resulting in possible nervousness, PSTD, high blood pressure, heart problems and depression. Did your mother suffer from any addictions? This could include alcohol, smoking, food and medication.

Discussed in Volume 1: Activity / Sports fanatic, Alcoholism, Arguing, Baking / Cooking, Bathing, Cheese, Cigarettes (see Smoking), Cocaine, Coffee / Coca Cola, Collecting, Computer Games, Crime – petty (e.g. shoplifting), Crime – stealing, Crime – violent, Crystal meth, Dairy, Food (see Weight Problems), Glue (inhaling glue), Heroin, Laughter (compulsive nervous laughter), LSD, Marijuana, Relationships, Sedatives, Sex Addiction.

Addison's Disease

See Adrenals, Fever, Muscle Problems, Nausea

Emotions

You have dissociated from any goals and emotions causing you to feel out of sync with yourself and those around you. You feel uncertain about life, your future as well as the direction that life is taking you in. You feel controlled by outside influences and are unable to stand strong with your own power.

Adenoids

See Lymphatic Filariasis, Lymphatic System Compromised

Emotions

You feel that you are always in trouble and are to blame for everything that goes wrong. You have been manipulated to such an extent, that you're very vulnerable to being used as the scapegoat for other people's mistakes. Parents and influential people often project their resentment and bitterness towards you in an effort to rid themselves of their frustration. You may have a parent who is jealous of the attention you receive from others.

Adjustment Disorder

See Anxiety, Depression, Seasonal Adjustment Disorder (SAD), Post-Traumatic Stress Disorder (PTSD)

Emotions

You may often feel challenged to adapt to new changes in your environment. You may have had an emotionally unstable or unpredictable childhood with your peaceful state and safety regularly disturbed by trauma such as physical or emotional abuse, bullying or sudden dramatic changes.

Adoption

Emotions

Your intimate relationships often don't last long due to feeling worthless and self-sabotaging patterns. You often overcompensate for feeling thrown away by holding on too strongly to a partner in fear of being abandoned again. This possessive behavior also allows you to hold onto unhealthy relationships far longer than you should, as you would much rather be with someone than be alone. You often have a great fear of not belonging anywhere.

Adrenals

See Addison's Disease, Cushing's Disease, Congenital Adrenal Hyperplasia (CAH)

Adrenals Right Side: You crave power however; you often resist being put in a position of power, as the price you'd pay would be too high. More detail is discussed in Volume 1.

Adrenals Left Side*:* You feel disappointed in a female figure, which is a role model. This role model may have passed away which made you feel abandoned or having regret in being unable to express any possible grievances with this person. Emotions common for Depleted and Overactive Adrenals are discussed in Volume 1.

Adrenoleukodystrophy ALD discussed in Volume 1.

Aglactia

See Breastfeeding

AIDS / HIV

See Attacked, Blood, Kaposi Sarcoma, Suicide, Virus

Emotions

The consciousness of the virus can influence the body, just like any parasite that invades. You might be feeling emotions such as, "You need me." You have trouble differentiating who is a friend and who is an enemy. Your self-loathing and low self-esteem has led you on a path of self-destruction. You seem to be searching for a way out of life (not necessarily by death, more so by making big and drastic changes).

Alcoholism

See Addictions, Anxiety, Birth (Caesarean), Cirrhosis, Depression, Fetal Alcohol Syndrome, Malnutrition, Osteoporosis, Panic Attack, Pellagra, Senility

Emotions

Alcoholism general: If you were abused as a child then abuse and trauma become normal; you grow accustomed to abuse. As a result, you may unconsciously attract and recreate the abusive circumstances experienced during childhood. You are often drawn to circumstances and people that remind you of the childhood trauma, as it feels familiar and normal. In a way, you may often feel safer when in destructive circumstances as at least you know how to survive.

More information and more on being an Abusive Alcoholic are discussed in Volume 1.

Allergies

See Celiac Disease, Hives, Lactose Intolerance, Rash, Sinus, Skin Problems

Emotions

You are experiencing hostile feelings towards an invasive / offensive partner, family or environment. You may be suppressing deep grief due to a controlling and dominating childhood, which left you feeling very insecure and unsure of your position within the family. Due to poor personal boundaries, you feel very offended by people who have flamboyant or invasive personalities.

Discussed in Volume 1: Bee Sting, Bread / wheat / gluten, Dairy, Nuts, Penicillin, Pepper, Pollen, Shellfish (see also Hives), Soap, Sun, Yeast.

Alopecia

See Eczema, Fungus, Hair-Loss, Tinea Capitis

Emotions

Feeling disconnected from your feminine / masculine power is often the main issue with this condition. You might dress and groom yourself well however, you cannot connect to the image that you project to the world. Can you feel in yourself what others see, such as when you receive a compliment? You are not allowing yourself to make your own decisions and choices in life. People often dictate to you, which make you feel resentful and unable to express clear boundaries. You feel that you are being treated like a child or someone who is helpless, making you feel undermined, resentful and determined to prove your ability to cope and be strong. There was a lack of emotional freedom during your childhood to freely choose for yourself and make your own decisions. Instead, you had to adhere to the choices made by a stressed out mother, father or caretaker. You may have been emotionally manipulated or physically abused (this is often more related to grandparents and ancestry).

Alzheimer's Disease

See Dementia, Huntington's Disease, Multiple Personality Disorder (MPD

Emotions

You often feel challenged by your intense emotions such as resentment, anger or old grudges that are keeping out of sight. You may feel challenged when faced with a situation that would require you to let go of an old hurt. You feel "done in" by the illness and dominating people in your past. You feel that others didn't nurture you in a way that you wanted to be nurtured and loved.

Amebiasis / Amoebiasis

See Digestive Problems, Parasites

Amnesia

See Accident, Concussion

Emotions

Amnesia could start as a way to escape taking responsibility. You may have already experienced an enormous sense of feeling responsible due to a parent's / partners / co-workers actions or manipulations. You most likely have experienced abuse in your life. You could be on the tipping edge of becoming the abuser yourself as a result of overcompensating for being bullied or abused during childhood.

Amyotrophic lateral sclerosis (ALS)

See Kennedy's Disease, Motor Neuron Disease

Anal Problems

See Bleeding, Colon Cancer, Digestive Problems, Hemorrhoids, Intestines, Prolapsed Bowels, Rectum

Emotions

Anal problems often stem from issues going on outside your life, in your environment or with relationships. You may be unable to let go of your anger and resentment toward the past and the circumstances that you've had to tolerate. You feel safe holding on to your trauma and emotions because you fear if you let go of the trauma, some other trauma may take its place. You often feel painfully insecure and overly sensitive toward others and your environment. As a result, you feel very irritated, intimidated or frustrated, as you want to take leadership but lack the confidence.

Anal Cancer

See Cancer section as well. You may have suppressed anger and resentment that has reached a point where it is out of control and needs to be dealt with as soon as possible. More information in Volume 1.

Anal Itching

See Parasites section as well. You cannot let go of past experiences that caused you a great deal of grief. More information in Volume 1.

Anal Bleeding

See Bleeding Problems, Prolapsed Bowels. You feel challenged when faced with circumstances in which you need to forgive people that have caused you harm or taken advantage of you. More information in Volume 1.

Anal Abscesses

See Abscess. There is often an unwillingness to let go of anger. You are stewing in your frustration and irritation—emotions that have been building up for a long time. More information in Volume 1.

Anaphylaxes

See Allergies, Attacked, Auto Immune, Bites

Emotions

Your family environment may have been dramatic; everything was turned into a crisis. You felt stuck in an environment where people created superficial stress, which left you anxious and tense. Your immune system feels challenged due to stress in the environment. There is often trauma related to feeling caught up in unpredictable circumstances and people.

Anemia

See Acute Lymphoblastic Leukemia, Crohn's Disease, Circulation Problems, Blood, Fatigue, Lactic Acidosis, Sickle Cell

Emotions

Anemia can start in many ways. One way is due to blood loss. You may feel that a parasitic person or circumstance that is beyond your control has drained your life force out of you. You have experienced circumstances that were exhausting and traumatic but feel challenged as to how to process this tension. Stress and anger as emotional outbursts are not tolerated. You often feel stuck in fight or flight mode and this is taking a toll on you; emotionally, physically and mentally.

Anesthesia

See Birth, Pregnancy

Emotions

The longer it takes for the anesthesia to be released by the body, the more in need you are of a break from stress and responsibilities in your life. It begs the question, why didn't you exercise clear boundaries so that your body and mental state didn't feel so depleted?

Anorexia

See Anxiety, Depression, Digestive Problems, Malnutrition, Marasmus

Emotions

You don't believe that anyone would ever think you are beautiful. You feel there is always something wrong with your body and you will go to extreme lengths to correct it by cutting off food intake. This could be due to a childhood where you were exposed to excessive criticism by influential people, shaping you into becoming who you are. You often feel like a failure who is not good enough. You do not feel accepted by those closest to you, leaving you with a great deal of emptiness. In comparing yourself to others, you raise your personal standards to often unrealistic goals. When you fail to reach these lofty standards, it only reinforces your low self-esteem.

The result is that you feel unworthy and do not respect your body or your needs.

Anxiety

See Arrhythmia, Adjustment Disorder, Depression, Nervous Breakdown, Obsessive-Compulsive Disorder, Panic Attack, Post-Traumatic Stress Disorder (PTSD), Seasonal Adjustment Disorder (SAD), Separation Anxiety, Speech, Stuttering

Emotions

Anxiety is caused by unresolved trauma that has piled up. The anxiety is surfacing to push you to change certain patterns and resolve unresolved problems. Anxiety can sometimes take the form of excessive worrying, feeling a sense of urgency, panic or mild paranoia. You may find yourself restless, edgy or tense, having difficulty sleeping and your mind racing from one thought to another. You often worry about everyday things, such as work, finances and family. You don't know when to relax and when it's valid to worry.

Anxiety (Separation Anxiety)

See Anxiety, Depression, PTSD, Birth (Placenta), Hyperventilation, Panic Attack

Emotions

You often feel stressed when separated from a loved one, caretaker or familiar group. If the client is a child then it's common for a child to experience this when they spend the majority of their time with one primary care taker and are then separated from this person. Separation anxiety can start when the mother or fulltime caretaker begins a fulltime job elsewhere and needs to leave the child with someone else. It could also develop when babies are left in a room to cry themselves to sleep on a regular basis. In most cases, the anxiety is short lived. Symptoms can include continuous crying, irritability, poor appetite, sleeplessness, and moodiness or compulsive behavior.

Apnea

See Anemia, Fatigue, Narcolepsy, Sleep Disorders

Emotions

You often felt suppressed in a family who demanded too much of you. Your relationship with your mother may have run hot and cold—leaving you with a cup that is always half full. Often the attention and love would leave you confused and uncertain of your self-worth.

Appendicitis

See Colon, Digestive Problems, Inflammation / Infections

Emotions

A burst appendix can have fatal consequences. This begs the question - why are you attacking yourself in this way? What circumstances have grown out of control? Whom and what circumstances in your life do you now hate or resent?

Arrhythmia

See Anxiety, Heart Problems

Emotions

You are often "holding your breath" as you think something bad is going to happen at any minute. It is best to always be prepared for the worst. In childhood, you never knew where you stood with anyone. Behavior of loved ones was never consistent. Your guard is up and on full alert. You feel unsupported and sense that there is danger everywhere, except most people don't realize it. This leaves you in charge of looking out for everyone else. You are the one who takes care of everything, making sure all is well.

Artery Problems

See Atherosclerosis, Blood, Blood Clot, Cardio-Vascular Problems, Heart Problems, Hypertension, Vasculitis, Vein Problems, Thrombosis

Emotions

Arteries reflect how people carry themselves in public. How they communicate with others. This condition is also related to the ability to be in the flow of life and how in sync you are with your job, family and personal relationships. You often feel challenged when trying to communicate your emotions and boundaries. You think you express yourself clearly but the reality is your listeners often don't understand what you're saying. Somehow, the message you prepare in your mind does not translate. This is often due to a childhood in which you were suppressed and not allowed to complete your sentences and fully express any opinions.

Arthritis

See Bursitis, Carpal Tunnel Syndrome, Inflammation, Joint Problems, Nerve Problems, Pelvic Problems, Reactive Arthritis, Rheumatoid Arthritis, Sickle Cell, Tendon Problems

Emotions

This condition is brought on by inflammation in the joints. You may be very rigid in your life or relationships, tightly controlling your emotions. You draw your power and strength from being stubborn. Stubbornness served you very well during childhood. You are often reluctant to ask for support. Your pride keeps you from leaning on others, which you think of as a weakness. You have been fending for yourself for a long time. You can be self-critical and self-destructive. You feel restricted in your circumstances and don't seem to feel that you can speak your mind. This leaves you feeling bitter toward the people you feel controlled and silenced by.

Asbestos

See Asbestos, Cancer

Emotions

You do not attend to your own needs. You may have surrounded yourself with unhealthy relationships that restrict you from being yourself. Let go of your, "I am fine" façade and be who you truly want to be. This stems from not feeling accepted by family or peers.

Asphyxiating Thoracic Dystrophy (ATD)

See Congenital Disorders

Asthma

See Fibromyalgia, Lungs, Toxins

Emotions

Adult sufferers take on too much stress and responsibility. It is now important to take control of your life. You may have trouble coping with stressful circumstances and can easily get overwhelmed. You were often made to feel incompetent when trying to do things on your own. You feel too attached to someone (often a parent) and may be feeling this person's grief, stress, annoyance or strain. It is an overwhelming experience for you, as you may not recognize you're expressing someone else's stress and fears. Do you feel your lungs tightening when a parent is angry or upset?

Atherosclerosis

See Arteries, Blood, Cholesterol, Weight Problems

Emotions

You often felt attacked (either verbally or physically) and criticized when you communicated any needs or expressed yourself. As a result, you feel deeply fearful of speaking up. You may feel a great need to buffer yourself against the harsh communication of others. You have turned inward trying to find comfort within. This hiding instinct has been activated by your circumstances.

Athetosis / Athetoid discussed in Volume 1

See Abasia, Chorea, Muscle Problems, Tic, Tremor

Emotions

Athletes Foot

See Fungus, Rashes, Parasites, Skin Problems

Emotions

You are walking through life feeling resentful, disempowered and irritated by influential people and circumstances. You often use resentment to express boundaries. You are unhappy with the direction your life is heading and the criticism you are receiving. You are irritated by influential people who have not respected your boundaries or given you the emotional space you need in order to grow.

Atlas Problems

See Back Pain, Headache, Migraine, Shoulder Pain, Spinal Cord Problems

Emotions

You feel that life is hard and that is how it should be. Your rigidity is sabotaging new opportunities and phases that are revealing itself in your life. New phases will be challenging, as a result it's easier to avoid personal progress. There is a desire to move forward, yet your negative association with change is often holding you back.

It begs the question, "What happened in your life during times of change when you started something new (a goal or project)?"

Attacked discussed in Volume 1.

Attention Deficit Hyperactivity Disorder ADHD

See Anxiety, Depression, Post-Traumatic Stress Disorder (PTSD),

Emotions

Your body may have experienced a great deal of trauma during birth. In utero you may have felt affected by your mother's hormones and anxiety. You often don't want to be too attached to people around you and choose to hide your vulnerabilities and sensitivity with a big, outgoing personality. You may have a fear of being ashamed and blamed, regardless of whether you did something wrong or not. You feel that you were blamed for many mistakes that weren't your fault. No matter how much you protested your innocence, you were not believed. Your family life has been stressful and you're not always sure where you stand with your parents, often feeling like an odd one out.

Autism

See Attack, Toxins

Emotions

You may have experienced a great deal of fear (being out of control) and anxiety to such an extent that you completely disconnected yourself from everything around you. You feel under attack by the environment surrounding you such as people, toxins or circumstances that are unhealthy. You feel out of control and frustrated, as you cannot completely control your body. You feel ashamed of your condition—you are aware of the hurtful words and reactions of people around you. You often feel like a puppet that is being controlled by an invisible hand, which results in a feeling of powerlessness. Overwhelming emotions make you feel challenged and out of your depth The environment merely triggered this condition that seemed to have been inactive. A previously inactive trauma has recently been triggered. A trauma from this lifetime may have activated a suppressed ancestral pattern or trauma. This may be subtle, yet have a big impact.

Auto Immune Disease

See Addison's, Arthritis, Attacked, Diabetes, Hypoglycemia, Immune System, Lupus, Multiple Sclerosis, Thyroid, Virus

Emotions

There are times when you feel challenged to judge for yourself, "Who is my friend and who is my enemy?" You don't trust your own judgment or those around you whom you rely on. You may be stuck in an unconscious state of flight or fight. You seem to feel under attack (either verbally or physically) by others. You don't feel comfortable or welcome in the family.

You often confuse positive criticism with a personal attack—always looking for signs in communication that an attack is imminent. You expect the worst-case scenario and are prepared for it.

Back Problems

See Atlas Problems, Bone Cancer, Cumulative Trauma Disorder, Lower Back Pain, Middle Back, Multiple Scoliosis, Muscle Problems, Myofascial Pain Syndrome (MPS), Osteoporosis, Paget's Disease, Pain, Shoulder Problems, Slipped Disc, Spinal Cord Problems, Spinal Stenosis, Upper Back, Scoliosis, Skeletal System

Emotions

You feel that you have to guard everything that is important to you in life. You may also feel that the tension in your body keeps you safe and protects you from experiencing further trauma. The tension and rigidity is almost a boundary. When you feel rigid and tensed, it is easier to resist and push unpleasant circumstances and people away. The tension acts as a buffer between you and others. The tension is also often a freeze instinct that was activated during a very stressful time in your life. You may feel a great deal of shame in public due to a lack of confidence and fear of being humiliated. You often lack support in life, as the support others give is not necessarily the kind of support you need.

Back – Calcification of Muscles

You are doing something in your life that doesn't resonate with you, carrying a great deal of responsibility or seeing a project through to the end. You feel obligated to help and serve others, which may be a pattern you copied from a parent.

Back (Upper Back)

See Accidents, Back Pain

Emotions

You have heard enough of others opinions and want to follow your own path and stick to your own opinion. If only you could figure out what that is! People have projected their own personal agenda onto you in the past. This may have resulted in only hearing what you want to hear, which is known as selective hearing.

Shoulder-blades

See Pain

Emotions

You are pushing against expectations that have been projected onto you. You feel a lack of freedom in your life. You feel you have to pretend to be strong and you are burdened by this façade. You often feel obligated to do things you don't enjoy, turning every task into a burden.

Back (Middle Back)

See Accidents, Back Pain

Emotions

You feel unable to escape feelings related to sadness and depression. Bad times now overshadow the good times. Others needs are more important than your own. You are losing sight of your personal progress and feel like you have no role in life, just missed opportunities.

Back (Lower Back)

See Accidents, Back Pain

Emotions

Lower back problems are often an indication of financial problems and feeling financially responsible for others. Pain here is triggered when there is no clear structure in your financial affairs. You may feel confused as to what your responsibilities are and what they should be. You often feel burdened by keeping the peace and balance in the household. You may lack discernment as to when you should act as a provider, when to emotionally support and when to just be a facilitator and supporter.

Discussed in Volume 1: Fused lower spine for women men separately.

Coccyx Problems

See Accidents, Pain, Spinal Cord Problems

Emotions

You have been made to feel responsible for problems that are now in the past but you are still holding on to guilt. You may give and never receive—your self worth is tied into how much you can do for others. You don't feel deserving of the same love and attention you give to others. You are subject to someone else's controlling nature, keeping you from settling into your environment or moving on to the next phase of your life.

Bacteria

See Chlamydia, E.Coli, Inflammation, Parasites, Septicemia

Emotions

When you explore a situation that involves bacteria then are you are often searching for issues related to guilt, regret, self-punishment, conflict within the environment or taking on too much responsibility. You often feel overwhelmed with responsibilities that may be causing a great deal of conflict within you or with people in your life.

Bell's Palsy

See Nerve Problems, Paralysis

Emotions

You may have experienced a very stressful childhood that made you feel out of control, disrespected and walked over. Your low self-esteem allows others to walk all over you. You have mastered the ability to rigidly control your emotions such as anger, resentment or lack of trust. This also includes feelings of revenge. As a result of this pattern, you find it challenging to judge how stressful, abusive, invasive and traumatic your circumstances were and perhaps still are. Your threshold for enduring abusive circumstances becomes higher and higher overtime.

Discussed in Volume 1: Right side paralyses and left side paralyses discussed in Volume 1.

Bi-Polar (Manic Depression)

See Anxiety, Depression, Schizophrenia

Emotions

You may have experienced long-term abuse and have reached the end of your rope. This abuse can include emotional, mental or physical abuse. You feel a great deal of resentment as people walk over you due to poor personal boundaries. This has left you feeling extremely angry and enraged. Your anger is your way of overcompensating for the lack of control you've had throughout life. You defend yourself by means of expressing anger and rage whenever you feel threatened. You often launch verbal attacks with the intention to ward off people.

Birth

See Abortion, Estrogen Problems, Fallopian Tube Problems, Hysterectomy, Labor Pain, Ovary Problems, Pregnancy, Uterus Problems

Anesthesia during birth

Emotions

You may feel incompetent, inadequate or numb toward others and life. You find it challenging to receive love and nurturing. The anesthesia may have created a great deal of confusion towards your mother during birth. You were unable to feel and find comfort or security from your mother during the birth. More information is discussed in Volume 1.

Birth Pain

Emotions

There is often a collective consciousness that implies that childbirth will be very painful. Many mothers have reported that they gave their power away due to horror stories about childbirth. This created more fear and tension in the body. They were convinced that they would have an awful and painful birth. In most cases, that is exactly what happened. More information is discussed in Volume 1.

Breech Birth

Emotions

You are here to assist people in their relationships with others and themselves. You may test people's boundaries and make them think twice about certain aspects in their lives. You may be very spiritual. You help people look at themselves in completely different ways—you are a soul-searching kick-starter! You can be very impulsive when making decisions. More information is discussed in Volume 1.

Caesarean

Emotions

Children born via caesarean often find it challenging to connect and fully experience their emotions. This is often as a result of drugs that were used during the caesarean process. The mother's emotions also have an impact on the child. How did the mother feel when the procedure was taking place? How did her emotions affect you when she felt pain from the procedure? More information is discussed in Volume 1.

Delayed Labor (deliberate)

Emotions

You often battle with emotions such as feeling controlled, feeling held back or out of control. These emotions are a result of your unresolved birth trauma. This may also be an overlap of your mother's stress and your stress during the birth process. You may have felt frustrated and anxious, as you felt blocked from moving through the birth canal. The pressure in the baby's head builds up and more pressure is placed on the neck, shoulders, chest and upper back area. This creates a great deal of discomfort for the baby. More information is discussed in Volume 1.

Forceps / Vacuum Birth

Emotions

A person who was born with the assistance of forceps often feels overwhelmed very quickly in their day to day to life. It may feel that you are being pulled in all directions at once. You often find it challenging to complete tasks and projects. You sabotage your progress as your birth process (also seen as a project) was interrupted and sabotaged. There was an interference with the baby's ability to complete their birth. This may result in you feeling that you do not have freedom of choice as someone might always interfere with your affairs. More information is discussed in Volume 1.

Incubator Babies
Emotions

You feel isolated and abandoned—often disconnected from your source of nurturing and safety. This causes anxiety and abandonment trauma. You may feel that you can never have enough of what you need as you were disconnected from your mother and source of food (breast milk) after birth. More information is discussed in Volume 1.

Induced Labor for the Mother
Emotions

You are experiencing a mixture of emotions. You are so exhausted and stressed that you may have stopped caring about why you wanted the child in the first place. You may be unconsciously second guessing your intentions and ability to be a good mother. Did you conceive to please a partner? Did you conceive to save a marriage or relationship? Did you conceive to give your life more meaning? Is the timing right to have a child in these current circumstances / lifestyle? More information is discussed in Volume 1.

Induced Labor for the Baby
Emotions

You often feel pushed far beyond your boundaries and limits. The baby is very aware of the mother's emotions. There seems to be a blurred line between the baby's stress and the mother's stress. You may be associating life, changes and feeling under pressure with your mother's emotions. Stressful circumstances may trigger the stress that you experienced during birth; along with triggering your mother's emotions, which you may have copied during birth. More information is discussed in Volume 1.

Missing Twin
Emotions

The missing twin has often been traced back to being the umbilical cord that was cut off. The baby was disconnected from the placenta which was perceived as another living being / organ in the womb. Disconnection from the placenta results in the baby feeling that they have lost a part of themselves and that there was a twin with them in the womb. They feel that the other twin didn't make it. This may result in grieving for someone that was supposed to be in his or her life. This grief often stays with a person for the rest of their life, if not correctly processed and healed. It also results in feeling, "People will leave me behind; people will never stick around in my life." More information is discussed in Volume 1.

Natural Vaginal Birth
Emotions

Natural birth with no complications would always be the ideal birth. This allows the baby to define their physical boundaries. You were able to experience a natural process of being squeezed stimulating all necessary areas on your body and organs. It is still important though to explore how your mother felt during birth especially if it was her first birth and how her trauma and stress affected you. More information is discussed in Volume 1.

Oxygen Deprivation

Emotions

You may feel attacked and unwelcomed by life. You often feel that you have intruded on other people's lives. You didn't feel ready to face your life contract and the people in it, knowing that you were not meant to come so early.

Placenta

Emotions

Separation from the placenta could result in a child needing a security blanket or toy to replace the connection and attachment they had to the placenta. You found comfort in the placenta during the womb stages. Once you were separated, the separation anxiety may have kicked in and you needed a substitute for the missing placenta.

Premature Birth

Emotions

You have had enough of your womb environment and want to get out. There may have been toxicity or a threat, such as illness of your mother, from which you needed to escape. Your mother's emotional state may also have had a big impact on you. It is important to remember that negative and powerful emotions might feel normal to an adult. They may have built-up a high threshold for intense emotions. For a developing fetus, it can feel extremely intense to experience tension from the mother as a result of her negative emotions. Long-term stress or unhealthy conditions of the mother and her environment may result in the fetus wanting to escape their environment. More information is discussed in Volume 1.

Discussed in Volume 1: Working with the mother that gave birth to a premature baby and with the client that was born premature.

Prolonged / Delayed Labor

Emotions

Your mother may have been told by her female family members that they all had a very long and painful labor. This inevitably became stuck in the back of her mind leading to a sense that she was doomed for a similar labor experience. You feel stuck in life and often find yourself in unhappy circumstances. You often unconsciously create circumstances in which you feel stuck and trapped with no way out. More information is discussed in Volume 1.

Rumination Syndrome / Merycism

See Nausea, Rumination Syndrome

Umbilical Cord (Strangled)

Emotions

You often feel that you have to fight against people and your circumstances. Nurturing and love felt toxic (especially if your mother had a bad diet or abused substances). You are often dramatic and see things in black or white - there is no in between. You feel attacked (either verbally or physically) and suffocated in confrontational situations. You often feel challenged when you need to express emotions. As a result, you tend to cut yourself off from others and emotionally dissociate from relationships. More information is discussed in Volume 1.

Unwanted Birth (baby conceived by accident)

Emotions

Unwanted births can be traumatic for both mother and child. Your mother may have decided to keep you due to fear of rejection, being judged, ridiculed or abandoned by her family. She may also have kept you because of religious reasons. She often projects hostility and rejection toward you. This is accompanied by a great deal of guilt, humiliation and feeling like a failure. Your mother may resent the fact that she will have to give up and change a part of her life due to a mistake. You may feel like a mistake and not good enough in your mother's presence. More information is discussed in Volume 1.

Womb
Emotions

The fetus can experience discomfort, tension and even stress when the mother is in pain or in circumstances that cause her great stress. The fetus does not experience trauma the same way as the mother. What is important here is to explore how the trauma that affected your mother influenced you in utero. More information is discussed in Volume 1.

Bites

See Anaphylaxes, Attack
Emotions

You may have felt under attack (either verbally or physically) by circumstances or by someone in your surroundings. Your personal space has often been disrespected and invaded by a dominant figure in your life. You have a fear of challenging those people who have a powerful influence in your life.

Bladder Problems

See Bladder Cancer, Candida, Inflammation, Interstitial Cystitis, Urethritis, Urinary Incontinence
Emotions

People store a great deal of their daily emotional irritations in their bladder and in the urinary tract. When a person is overwhelmed with a lot of stress, irritation or feeling pissed off, it can physically surface in these areas. Bladder problems often start when a person is trying really hard to resist being controlled by an authority figure. This could be a boss, mother, father or sibling. You feel a great deal of anger toward someone that is challenging you. Because you feel unsafe expressing yourself towards this person, you often revert to aggression in order to emotionally protect yourself. Your fear of being ridiculed, punished or attacked makes you project aggression. The aggression forms a buffer between you and an abuser or influential person that is challenging your self-worth or territory.

Bladder Cancer, discussed in Volume 1.

See Bladder, Cystitis

Bleeding

See Anal Problems, Endometriosis, Hemorrhaging, Ovary
Emotions

You may feel like giving up in many areas of your life—you feel like all hope is lost. Your values in life are not acknowledged, respected or validated. You are dwelling on your unresolved past and it is eating away at you. Stubborn people, who are unwilling to cooperate and compromise with you, meet your need for support with opposition and jealousy. More information is discussed in Volume 1.

Blindness

See Cataracts, Diabetes, Eye Problems, Paget's Disease

Emotions

Life has become too dramatic and stressful. You don't want to see what is going on around you anymore. It may be that if you can't see it, it won't upset you. You carry a great deal of resentment about not being able to see. Mentally you feel exhausted and do not want to participate in stressful circumstances. You are in need of a new, stress free experience. More information is discussed in Volume 1.

Blisters

See Canker Sores, Cold Sores, Coxsackie Virus, Rashes, Rosacea

Emotions

You often make things hard for yourself, struggling with a great deal of self-created stress, boundary failures or too many responsibilities. There is an underlying pattern of self-punishment. Suppressed anger is currently being triggered by another person or by circumstances. There is a constant problem that is irritating you and draining your energy; it must be dealt with.

Bloated

See Anxiety, Colitis, Colon Problems Intestines, Digestive Problems

Emotions

Along with food, you have been digesting strong emotions such as fear or anger about your current circumstances. You may be stressed out about a situation that feels unsolvable, out of your control. You often underestimate your ability to cope with the many tasks and demands from others. It is difficult for you to express your boundaries. Because you don't always know what you want, you often follow other's dreams and goals rather than your own. Your childhood may have been stressful, filled with anxiety that has been hard to cope with. As a result, whenever a current event triggers a past trauma, you find it challenging to deal with. Being still and quiet has always kept you out of harm's way

Blood discussed in Volume 1.

See Anemia, Blood Clot, Bruises High Blood Pressure, HIV / AIDS, Hypertension, Leukemia, Low Blood Pressure, Melanoma, Sepsis, Sickle Cell, Thrombosis

Blood Clot / Coagulation

See Arteries, Blood, Veins

Emotions

You are at wits end and feel that there is no love left in your life. A challenging relationship has run its course and you feel exhausted and drained by life, work or family responsibilities. You often feel weighed down by responsibilities. You are often seen as the person who has to keep it all together on behalf of everyone else. Your body is not willing to be pushed so hard anymore and is in need of a break. You seem to feel you have to accept things as they are but by not communicating your boundaries, you are feeling suffocated by your circumstances.

Blood Poisoning

See Blood, Poisoning, Toxins

Emotions

You feel poisoned by the false intentions of others. You may have made an association that it is not safe to ask for love and attention. You feel disappointed having learned the full extent of what is really going on in your environment—the curtain has pulled back to reveal all of your vulnerabilities. You don't trust others, believing that everyone has a hidden agenda. As a result, you tend to avoid personal relations and interactions with people.

Blood Pressure High

See Blood, Pineal Gland Problems, Pituitary Gland Problems

Emotions

You feel powerless in your circumstances and use suppressed rage, aggression or anger to express boundaries. You fear being out of control and as a result, end-up feeling overly controlling of others and situations. You may still be grieving due to a lack of love from your parents, always on the search for more love. There seems to have been a great deal of stress in childhood that has not been resolved. This may have caused you to feel defensive as an adult, with the intention of keeping yourself safe. You like to be in control, which is your way of overcompensating for a lack of control in childhood.

Blood Pressure Low

See Blood, Pituitary Gland Problems

Emotions

You have allowed yourself to be weakened by life and harsh interactions with family. You didn't have enough support, motivation and praise in order to build your confidence. As a result, you often doubt your ability to achieve your goals and become successful. You feel that no matter how hard you try, success is just out of your grasp. You often throw in the towel half way through projects.

Blood Transfusion

See Accident, Attack, Blood Problems

Emotions

You may feel criticized, under attack (either verbally or physically) or deeply angry due to the lack of respect you receive from other people. Your source of energy and inner strength feels depleted by old burdens, which leaves you feeling vulnerable or fed-up when confronted with new challenges.

Boils

See Acne, Bacteria, Skin Problems

Emotions

You often feel rejected and attacked by people that are projecting their insecurities at you.

You desperately want to trust others, but have felt betrayed whenever you've given someone the benefit of the doubt. You want to receive acceptance from the people that have rejected or abandoned you; often these are family members and loved ones. You have a love-hate relationship with family, partners or friends that trigger self-loathing and low self-esteem. You may feel that no one wants you to be happy because others have sabotaged your happiness with destructive behavior. Now you have become self-destructive and are sabotaging your own success and personal progress.

Bone Cancer

See Bones Broken, Cancer, Lung Cancer, Skeletal System

Emotions

It is important that you establish whether the bone cancer is the starting point of the cancer or if it's a secondary cancer. For example, cancer can start in the lung and then metastasize to the bone. If that is the case, then explore lung cancer first and then bone cancer. Your experiences in life may have left you feeling weak, vulnerable or unsupported due to years of suppressed stress, anger and lack of support, your emotional, mental and physical state feels weakened and exhausted. Your immune system has suffered as well. You may have felt defenseless and invaded by your circumstances. Influential people's demands and expectations resulted in a great deal of pressure for you, causing you to feel out of control.

Bone Marrow

Emotions

You feel unsafe and unprotected as a result of the lack of support you've received in life. You almost feel as if you've been thrown in the deep end. You felt unprotected due the harshness of your circumstances. You often feel as if you are reaching out for safety and support, but no one is available to meet your needs. This condition often starts when your parents have been consumed by their own problems, thereby ignoring you emotionally. You may feel that you were left to fend for yourself without proper guidance. This made you feel like no one would ever look out for you.

Bone Problems / Broken

See Accident, Collarbone Problems, Concussion, Plantar Fasciitis, Skeletal System

Emotions

You often feel caught up in circumstances that make you feel resentful, pushed beyond your limits or out of your comfort zone. You've felt it necessary to suppress many talents and positive aspects in order to be accepted and respected by others. You often feel that your efforts are in vain. You feel that you are not good enough to just be yourself. You may feel that you always had to fight your own battles with no support, causing anger and resentment. You are now at a breaking point and feel like a failure.

Discussed in Volume 1: Broken arms or hands, Broken back, Broken legs, Dislocation (also see Shoulder Problems – Dislocation).

Botulism

See Alzheimer's Disease, Bacteria, Bells Palsy, Brain Cancer, Brain Tumor, Concussion, Head Ache, Huntington's Disease, Hypoxia, Mercury Poisoning, Migraine, Nerve Problems, Poisoning, Toxins

Emotions

You may feel invaded by people. The invasion can either be physical, emotional or by the environment or circumstances. You are trying to hold it all together with as much calmness as possible due to fear of upsetting someone that has the power to punish. You feel under tremendous pressure to perform and please others, often having to do things that you don't want to do. This may have left you feeling angry and unable to control the circumstances and outcome of your projects and goals. You seem to have many angry conversations going back and forth in your head mind. This stems from a long history of giving too much and not recognizing when to express healthy boundaries.

Brain Cancer

See Cancer

Emotions

You often feel conflicted between what your parents expect of you and what you actually want. On the one hand, doing what you want will not reward you with praise and the acknowledgment of your parents. Pleasing them always results in being loved and accepted. You give your power away and feel a loss of control in exchange for feeling loved and accepted. You don't express your needs, which makes you feel unworthy of having your own goals. You may have been made to feel guilty or wanting something other than what was expected of you. You want control of your own life, but feel obligated to obey authority. You feel pulled in two directions, leaving you angry and full of resentment. You may feel that influential people are controlling your destiny, delaying your personal progress. You have a fear that you will miss out on your special purpose in life.

Brain Tumor

See Acoustic Neuroma, Brain Cancer, Cancer, Tumor

Emotions

Stubbornness and being rigid about change are often the key words to explore. You seem to feel conflicted between what you want to believe and what you were taught to believe. You are often in a situation where you are pushed or manipulated to change. You may have had enough and now want to follow through on your own values, yet you feel guilty about letting go of childhood values and beliefs that were projected onto you. The more you mature, the more out of control you feel with your new found responsibilities and pressure from outside influences.

Breast Cancer

See Cancer, Lymphatic System Compromised

Emotions

You feel that you are the foundation of the family and hold it together, so you consider it necessary to project a strong façade toward the public, even if your private life is causing you great stress. You may find it challenging to grieve and show emotion due to fear of rejection and abandonment. In the past, expressing emotions may have made you look weak and as a result, you felt judged. You either suppress your emotions or it comes out in explosive ways that sets off more triggers such as anger, resentment and rejection or family disputes. Your outbursts only serve to push people away, leaving you feeling more abandoned. You may feel that communicating always comes at a great price. You often feel conflicted by what you need to say and the ramifications of it. You may associate expressing yourself with punishment and rejection.

Left breast

This often relates to your relationship with yourself, your mother, family and family responsibilities. Are you in conflict with your mother or your role as a mother? You may be in conflict with your partner over a child or family related issues.

Right breast

This often relates to your relationship with your father, leadership, trying to be strong or being brave during challenging times when everyone needs support.

Discussed in Volume 1: Cancer between the breasts, Breast Adenocarcinoma, Breast Melanoma, Intraductal carcinoma of the breast, Cancer of the milk ducts, Breast Tumor

Breast Cyst

See Cyst, Breast Cancer, Breast Problem

Emotions

You may have associated sexual pleasure with guilt, which makes you feel guilty and ashamed when you receive sexual attention from partners. There may also be a conflict between satisfying your sexual needs and the need to buffer yourself from sexual partners. This often stems from a childhood where touch was associated with punishment, abuse or invasion trauma. You may have been ashamed and made to feel guilty when you innocently explored sexuality as a child.

Breast Feeding

See Allergies / Milk, Pregnancy

Emotions

Not producing breast milk

This is often common when the mother finds it challenging to bond with the child, especially if it was an unexpected pregnancy or if it's the mother's first child. The new mother may feel awkward and inadequate in her new role. Often this is because the new mother herself didn't immediately feel a bond with her own mother when she was born and breast-fed. It also depends on whether the mother really did want the child. She might feel like the child intruded in her life, if the pregnancy was an accident.

Breast Problems

See Breast Cyst, Breast Feeding, Cyst, Lymphatic System Compromised

Emotions

You may have experienced an upbringing that involved your mother or another female authority figure causing you a great deal of stress. You feel challenged by the role of mother, wife or friend and what the expectations are. If you are a male then breast problems represent your sensitivity toward people's behavior towards you.

Breast Tumor

See Breast Cyst, Breast Problems, Tumors

Bronchitis

See Bacteria, Fever, Inflammation, Lung Problems,

Emotions

Bronchitis often starts when people overwork themselves, enduring long periods of stress. You feel challenged by the amount of guilt, regret or resentment you are holding on to. You feel that all your negative experiences have made you stronger; your strength is based on how much you have survived. This illusion of strength and testing your endurance comes at a price - you are exhausted.

Bruises

See Blood Problems, Circulation Problems, Skin Problems

Emotions

You accept criticism as a personal attack. You feel vulnerable within your current circumstances, as it may have triggered old hurt and trauma from the past, which you do not want to face. You are suppressing emotions that are coming to the surface because you have a fear of expressing yourself to a dominant parent or authority figure.

Bruxism

See Temporomandibular Joint and Muscle Disorder (TMJD) - Jaw Grinding / Clenching

Bulimia

See Anorexia, Digestive Problems, Malnutrition, Marasmus

Emotions

You may have been raised in a seemingly loving family however; there was conflict and hostility between family members behind closed doors. Affection and emotions that you were shown may have been very transparent and not sincere. Love that was demonstrated may have left you feeling disgusted, hostile or toxic.

Bunion

Emotions

You are stubborn and inflexible when faced with environmental and emotional changes. This stubbornness, determination and ability to endure hardships have become a source of strength. You often attract circumstances that will challenge your ability to cope and endure hardships. This serves as a reminder that you can overcome anything by drawing power from your stubbornness and unwillingness to conform to what is expected.

Burned

See Attack, Blisters, Skin Problems

Emotions

You feel you have been wrongfully blamed for something you are not responsible for. You may have been made to feel guilty and shameful whenever you expressed yourself. As a result, you prefer to respond to most situations with silence, only adding to your suppression cycle. You might be feeling guilty and ashamed because of negative thoughts towards someone who has upset you or treated you in an unjust manner. The anger has come to the surface and your cup is overflowing.

Bursitis

See Arthritis, Cramps, Foot Problems, Inflammation, Muscle Problems, Pelvic Problems, Tendon Problems

Emotions

I mentioned this paragraph under Arthritis, Cramps and Tendon section as a possible cause of this problem. It is important to explore in case it might be the underlying issue. You may not have had enough space to move around in the womb area due to lack of space or just not moving enough, leaving you stuck in one position for long periods of time. How did not having enough room to move make you feel? It is important to see if that feeling is the same as the one you have whenever your arthritis or arthritic pain is triggered. It is important to find the association you've made and how you felt at the time. Look past any superficial answer as these only represent secondary issues from the main core problem. You are searching for deep answers.

Calcification

See Muscle Problems, Shoulder Problems (Frozen Shoulder)

Emotions

You feel overly responsible for your loved ones in the role as partner, parent or authority figure. You feel that their emotional support alone is not good enough. All this may be a result of being under tremendous pressure to fix everything that was wrong in the family. You often take on extra responsibilities out of fear of rejection or not living up to the expectations of influential people in your life. In childhood, you were loved and praised when you took the role of an adult and met high expectations. Love was hard to come by and you had to work hard for the love you received.

Cancer

See Asbestos, Bladder Cancer, Brain Cancer, Breast Cancer, Chemo Therapy, Colon Cancer, Kaposi Sarcoma, Kidney Cancer, Liver Cancer, Lung Cancer, Lymphatic System Compromised, Lymphoma, Melanoma, Pancreatic Cancer, Prostate Cancer, Radiation, Skin Cancer, Skin Problems, Stomach, Toxins, Tumor

Emotions

You often experience people's actions and behavior toward you as invasive, aggressive or controlling. When you feel this way on a regular basis it may contribute to feeling powerless, angry, resentful or out of control. You may feel like a victim of circumstance. Your boundaries have been disrespected and you have reached a point where you are angry and resentful. You regret not setting clearer boundaries or standing up for yourself with loved ones. You spend time stewing over past mistakes, longing for things that should have taken place or choices you should have made. You often project a strong, cool and calm façade but under it all is a bubbling volcano. This facade has served you well over the years, keeping you safe from being exposed or vulnerable. You give too much of yourself, especially time and energy. You do not expect to receive in return—in fact, you feel that it is safer to give, in order to maintain control over the circumstances.

Candida

See Fungus, Immune System Compromised, Intestines, Digestive System, Dyspareunia

Emotions

You feel frustrated as you try to resolve a situation and approach a person that is causing you a great deal of irritation. You feel resentful toward people who do not need you anymore. If so, what is irritating you? People who have Candida have an outbreak or discharge (more and worse symptoms) when they feel anger and frustration toward someone or circumstances. It may also start when they feel exhausted and taken advantage of. You take pride in supporting people: being responsible and supporting others rewarded you with validation, love and acceptance.

Canker Sores

See Blisters, Cold Sores, Ulcers

Emotions

You may feel run down by your lifestyle. Because you do not value your time and often underestimate your ability to cope with so many responsibilities, you overburden yourself. This results in feeling anxious, stressed and tired. You loyalty to loved ones leaves you feeling obligated to push on, despite your lack of energy, time or resources. This self-sabotaging pattern takes a toll on the immune system. You feel drained and completely out of sync with your goals and relationships, unable to communicate your need for support. You may feel bitter and angry, or misunderstood whenever you communicate your opinions and concerns to another.

Cardiac Arrest

See Heart Problems

Cardio-Vascular Problems

See Heart Problems, Vein Problems

Emotions

You are all out of love, especially for yourself, as you have been giving and giving without expecting anything in return. Your inability to receive love has caused you to become strained and drained. In the past, you were rewarded for giving love and may have been made to feel ashamed when asking for love and support. This results in a secondary association with receiving, so that you feel your position in the family is more secure and more rewarded when you are of service to others.

Carpal Tunnel Syndrome

See Arthritis, Joint Problems, Muscle Problems, Myofascial Pain Syndrome (MPS), Nerve Problems, Tendon Problems, Wrist Problems,

Emotions

You feel rigid and stubborn when you are confronted with circumstances that would require you to ask for support and allow you to receive support. You often don't communicate your needs because of a fear of rejection, criticism or being considered a burden. You know exactly what you need but fear asking for support as you associate expressing your needs with being controlled. Your lack of self-expression may be holding you back from making personal progress and moving on with your goals. You may feel weighed down by responsibilities that have piled up as a result of not asking for support when you should.

Catalepsy

See Epilepsy, Muscle Problems, Pelvic Problems, Schizophrenia, Suicide,

Emotions

You are so set in your ways that you have almost become physically rigid and stagnant. You seem to be rebelling against changes taking place in your life. You have a great need to be different and unique and feel that that you will only be loved and noticed if you can become successful. There is conflict though as you are resistant to becoming successful due to a fear of failure and not feeling good enough. There is a deep-seated fear of being attacked, exposed or becoming vulnerable if you do succeed.

Cataracts

See Eye Problems

Emotions

You have not been able to see the hostility that was present during childhood until now. You are protecting yourself from feeling the lack of love that was present in your childhood and which may have been repeated in your marriage or other personal relationships. You were made to feel that others always had your best interest at heart, however you have since learned that people had selfish agendas. Realizing this may have caused you a great anguish, allowing a pattern of suppression to set in. There is often denial and a refusal to see and believe what your life foundation was built on.

Catarrh (Ear)

See Ear Problems, Inflammation

Emotions

You do not trust new information as a result of past negative experiences when influential people may have misled you. This left you feeling upset, disappointed or traumatized. There is a resistance (either conscious or unconscious) to take in new information, as you do not know whether it can be trusted. This pattern makes you resistant to opening yourself up to new possibilities and perspectives. There is a willingness to learn and listen to others, yet there always seems to be a distant voice in the back of your mind. This voice (fear) is a constant reminder of the disappointment or stress that was caused as a result of listening. You may be surrounded by arguments that are upsetting.

There is a resistance to hearing what is going on in your environment.

Celiac Disease

See Allergies, Intestines

Emotions

Acceptance, lack of acknowledgement, attention and love may have been hard to come by during childhood. Instead of having your needs met, you were often pushed too hard and left to feel that you couldn't do anything right. This made you work hard to achieve success, although you have now become addicted to pushing yourself for praise and acknowledgment. At the same time, you suppress feelings of emptiness and not feeling good enough or important enough. The secondary gain of pressuring yourself is that it allows you to avoid and deflect from deeper, more intense emotions and trauma. You often feel helpless and disempowered by influential people, feeling angry, frustrated and resentful. You feel frozen and trapped in current circumstances. Being controlled has become a way of life. Your identity and sexuality may have been suppressed and criticized by the opposite sex, which results in feeling powerless and stripped of any rights.

Cellulitis

See Inflammation, Skin Problems

Emotions

You may have become an angry, voiceless observer in your life. You learned from an early age to never challenge influential people, as you would only regret the consequences that would follow. You often feel unprotected by influential people in your life. As a result of your poor personal boundaries, you seem to feel responsible for too many chores and issues that are not your responsibility. This stems from a childhood where shame and guilt may have been used to manipulate. This may cause you to overcompensate, trying too hard to be accepted by others.

Cercarial Dermatitis (Swimmers itch)

See Allergies, Dermatitis, Parasites

Emotions

Someone or something is getting under your skin, getting the better of you. You feel challenged expressing clear boundaries but the more you hold back expressing boundaries, the more irritated, angry and resentful you become. There are times in your life when you feel, "This is not fair!" You may have been made to feel stupid, unworthy or inadequate when performing certain tasks. This may have challenged your ability to be utilized and feel successful. You often feel stuck and trapped in your circumstances. The flight instinct is activated yet you are unable to move away from a situation, which causes a great deal of irritation and helplessness.

Cerebral Palsy

See Bacteria, Meningitis, Nerve Problems, Virus

Emotions

After cerebral palsy started: You may feel directionless in life searching for a place to belong.

You often don't resonate with the people that are a part of your life. You feel dictated to without an option to make your own decisions, pulling you further from what you want to achieve in life. You feel like a victim of your poor personal boundaries. This is a repetitive cycle that surfaces in many areas of your life.

Cervical cancer

See Cancer, Female Problems, Pain, Pelvic Pain, Uterus Problems
Emotions
There are different options and approaches available when exploring this condition. One is that you may have a suppressed resentment toward men. Men seem to make you feel less superior, with no rights and no voice. You may feel invaded, disempowered or controlled by authority as a result of feeling powerless in the face of domineering authority figures. You feel that you have no right to stand your ground. Controlling, influential people may have disrespected your decisions as it related to your future and goals.

Chemical Poisoning

See Poisoning, Toxins

Chemotherapy

See Attacked (the body might feel under attacked by the radiation) Cancer, Radiation, Toxins
Emotions
Your body feels poisoned and under attack; physically challenged by the chemo. Chemo creates cell confusion as well as emotional confusion. Chemo often feels quite invasive, as if you are losing more control over the your health and bodily functions. It is important to explore earlier traumas related to poisoning and feeling under attack as well as feeling out of control.

Chest (Pressure) discussed in Volume 1.

See Anxiety, Heart Problems, Pain

Chicken Pox

See Immune System, Rashes, Shingles, Skin Problems, Virus
Emotions
If the client is a child: The client's mother may have felt challenged by her pregnancy and trusting her abilities to be a good mother. She felt challenged balancing the relationship between her, her husband and the newborn child. The mother had a low self-esteem possibly resulting in her not expressing clear boundaries. This caused her to suffer from self-created stress and frustrations. Her personal life and relations challenged how she felt about herself.

Chilblains

See Blisters, Inflammation, Rashes, Skin Problems
Emotions
You feel challenged when faced with circumstances that require you to trust authority figures and influential people who may have betrayed you. Your efforts were not praised and

appreciated in a fulfilling way, causing you to feel inadequate and destined for failure. There seems to be a self-sabotaging pattern in the family with matters related to the heart such as love and intimate relationships. You have seen evidence that love and unity is not safe, it is hostile and often unsupportive. You feel that the people who were supposed to protect you failed to do so, as you may have suffered from abuse during childhood. Your sincere efforts and kind nature were often taken advantage of, making your distrustful of the intentions of others. You take pride in your stubbornness and rigidity, as this is a source of strength and boundaries.

Chloasma

See Skin Problems, Vitiligo

Emotions

Trauma related to feminine beauty such as being and feeling beautiful. You may feel that you were not allowed to be more beautiful than your mother or a female authority. You may have an ancestral trauma where beautiful people were always attacked and abused. Your ancestor's appearances in the past may have attracted many problems and circumstances that resulted in them feeling out of control or invaded.

Chlamydia

See Bacteria, Infertility, Pain, Pelvic Problems

Emotions

You seem to have gone through a phase in your life where you've stopped caring about yourself. Your loved ones may have responded the same toward you at the time you were affected by this condition. You may not respect yourself and consequently attract people into your life who disrespect you, making you feel unworthy and useless. You are in conflict with your feminine or masculine qualities. Your gender makes you feel weak and prone to attract abuse from influential people. You are often willing to endure abusive and demeaning behavior at the hands of loved ones out of fear of loneliness.

Cholera

See Bacteria, Intestine (Small Intestine) Problems, Irritable Bowel Syndrome

Emotions

You feel a great deal of guilt and regret within your intimate relationships. Your parents may not have always had time for you in childhood, making you feel guilty for having and expressing emotional needs. You have had enough of guilt, regret and shame and are ready to rid yourself of these emotions and move forward in life.

Cholesterol (High)

See Atherosclerosis, Blood Problems, Chest Pressure, Heart Problems

Emotions

You seem to block love and joy from flowing into your life. Due to a fear of rejection, you often have trouble communicating your needs or truth to others. When you expressed any dislike in the past, you were often subjected to punishment. Bitterness and anxiety often go hand in hand with people that suffer from high cholesterol. You often overreact in confrontational circumstances that cause you to feel attacked (either verbally or physically). This is a result of pent up anger and frustration that causes you to feel overwhelmed and oversensitive to confrontation. This stems from a childhood where either parent could not control their emotions and would exaggerate their feelings when provoked. A parent may have over shared their stress, marriage problems or responsibilities with you during childhood. This may have caused you to feel helpless, scared and out of control.

Chorea

See Abasia, Athetosis, Nerve Problems, Tic, Tremor
This condition may also possibly start as a result of medication poisoning. See Poisoning and Toxins for more information.

Circulation Problems

See Dizziness, Heart Problems, Muscle Problems, Raynaud's Disease
Emotions
You suppress feeling positive emotions as you have made negative associations with joy and positive emotions. This pattern seems to have caused you to withdraw from your life, passions, goals and needs. You may not have had many opportunities to explore creativity as a child; instead, influential people often controlled how and when you expressed creativity.
   Discussed in Volume 1: Circulation problems in your hands, Circulation problems in your legs or feet

Cirrhosis

See Alcoholic, Liver, Toxins, Virus
Emotions
Your suppressed anger has grown out of control. You take everything personally as you feel responsible for any suffering around you. Every time you take a step or enter a new phase, you feel like you've already failed before you've begun. You are very set in your ways, causing you to become stagnant in many areas of your life. You have created a life filled with specific values, knowing what is right and wrong. Being rigid allows you to feel safe and you hold onto this even if it is the illusion of safety.

Coagulation

See Blood Problems, Blood Clot

Cold Sores

See Blisters, Canker Sores, Virus
Emotions
You seem to feel angry and deeply saddened by the things that you cannot say. You may be under the illusion that you have no right to speak up as a result of feeling suppressed during childhood. You feel run down by your responsibilities and the need to fight for what you want—nothing comes easily. You feel desperate to change circumstances and people in your life who cause you frustration. You do not feel heard or respected unless you lose your temper. You often choose partners who are strong willed, controlling and selfish, leaving you angry and feeling done in.

Colic

See Allergies, Anxiety, Crying, Digestive Problems
Emotions
You are a sensitive person who is having a hard time adjusting to a new environment. You might need to escape your current circumstances, yet you feel trapped and stuck. The mother and father might be annoyed, stressed, fatigued, anxious or angry and the baby is sensing this. Assist the mother and father as well to process their frustrations and to explore what is really upsetting them.

Colitis

See Colon Problems, Inflammation, Intestines, Irritable Bowel Syndrome
Emotions
You have been digesting food and emotions with anger and frustration. Circumstances in your present life triggered unpleasant and upsetting memories from the past. You often unconsciously create circumstances from which you need to be rescued from self-sabotaging patterns.

Collarbone Problems

See Back Problems, Bone Problems, Spinal Cord Problems
Emotions
The collarbone is about support and structure in a person's life. You seem to be pushing against circumstances that require you to change certain aspects of yourself that still serve you well. You are often resistant to change and feel held back by influential people from achieving your goals. You may believe that in order to achieve success, something needs to give. People usually support you in such a way that you feel controlled. Your association with support has been stressful, invasive, controlling or manipulative. As a result, you become stubborn when offered help because your stubbornness has kept you safe from controlling people in the past.

Colon Cancer

See Cancer, Colon Problems, Digestive Problems, Hernia, Intestine Problems, Irritable Bowel Syndrome IBS, Polyps
Emotions
You may have been made to feel stupid and inadequate at the expense of someone else's low self-esteem and bullying tactics. Influential people that feed off vulnerabilities and low self-esteem often target you. You have been blamed in such a way that caused you to fear making mistakes and being devalued. You were often at the receiving end of hostile love and emotional abuse when you expressed any emotional needs.

Colon Problems

See Colon Cancer, Digestive Problems, Diverticulitis, Inflammation / Infection, Polyps
Emotions
You do not want to let go of past negative experiences and trauma. You feel irritated and angry as a result of past experiences that you could not change or had no control over. You are still stewing over unresolved issues. You are pushing through challenging circumstances

on your own, making you feel overwhelmed, panicked or angry. You struggle as a result of self-created stress due to your stubbornness. Asking for support is not an option in your opinion, as people either fail to deliver or have unrealistic expectations in return for support. Being supported by people has made you feel controlled.

Concussion

See Bone Problems, Dizziness, Head Ache, Skeletal System, Tremor, Whiplash
Emotions
You should make more time to absorb and enjoy life. You may have become stuck indulging in the superficial side of life. You have moved away from your spirituality and your life has pushed you in a direction that does not resonate with your needs. You need to shift focus elsewhere, instead of concentrating on influential people's agendas and goals.

Congenital Disorders discussed in Volume 1.

Congestion

See Fever, Flu, Sinus

Conjunctivitis

See Eye Problems
Emotions
You feel in conflict with what you are seeing in life, causing you a great deal of anger. It may also be related to an irritating situation that has been brewing for a while in your personal life (often between family members). You have moved into a phase where you want to be left in peace. Your circumstances and environment is full of friction and you don't feel equipped with the right "tools" to deal with these circumstances. This causes you to feel stuck and helpless whenever you need to initiate any necessary changes in your life. You have become very sensitive and self-conscious of how others perceive you. You don't feel that you have what it takes to fit in with society; feeling shy, you want to withdraw from an environment that is often too intimidating.

Constipation

See Digestive Problems, Hernia, Intestines, Irritable Bowel Syndrome, Renal Disease
Emotions
You do not want to let go of your emotions. It is important to see that certain emotional patterns are serving you. You are afraid that if you let go then you might lose the stubborn qualities that have served you so well. You have internalized your emotions and need for love. Your desire to be accepted and receive love overrides your ability to express healthy boundaries. You take on too much at a time and when you need help or support, you often feel challenged asking for it. This often leaves you feeling resentful and unsupported. This pattern starts when you actually give what you need to others. You feel that you cannot manifest what you need as the focus is always directed at other's needs. You find your fulfillment through different types of behavior in public and adjust your character to suit the requirements needed to blend into social groups.

You often keep your own counsel, which causes you to have regular, explosive out bursts.

Coughing

See Bronchitis, Flu, Lung Problems

Emotions

You may have too many emotions bubbling to the surface and are too scared to express yourself. Your circumstances are irritating yet you feel powerless to make any changes. You feel controlled or pushed down by an influential person and you desperately want to get away from this situation. Your poor personal boundaries are keeping you from expressing yourself clearly.

Whooping Cough

You may feel that you are not allowed to express yourself freely. You have been made to feel guilty, ashamed or even punished for speaking up. This may have caused you to feel embarrassed when you communicate needs.

Coxsackie Virus discussed in Volume 1.

See Back Problems (lower back), Blisters, Fever, Meningitis, Muscle problems, Myofascial Pain Syndrome (MPS), Shoulder Problems, Virus

Crabs

See Parasites

Emotions

You seem to feel that your sexual needs are disgusting and unimportant—there is a great deal of guilt associated with your sexuality. You may feel that your partner's needs are more important than your own.

Cramps

See Arthritis, Bursitis, Digestive Problems, Intestinal Cramps, Muscle Problems, Myofascial Pain Syndrome (MPS), Tendon Problems, Toxins

Emotions

Cramps often start when you need to change patterns and habits that no longer serve you. You may have come from a family that believed that life is too serious to make time for fun. Those who work hard will be rewarded. You often feel that pleasure and freedom can only be found through hard work. You feel you only deserve pleasure and freedom after investing energy and time into projects. The catch is that you don't always recognize when to stop and how to establish healthy boundaries. You do not recognize when the body and mind needs a break. Your body is trying to let you know that you need to focus less on your future and more on your present life.

Crohn's Disease

See Anemia, Digestive Problems, Colon Problems, Ileitis, Intestines

Emotions

You grew up in a tug of war family dynamic. What you stood for was often challenged and demeaned by influential members of your family. This made you feel rejected and inadequate, as if you were not good enough during your childhood. You may have felt forced to always compromise with senior members of the family. You often felt that you were forced to understand another's point of view while your own views were dismissed. You enjoy being in the public eye although you have a fear of being exposed or losing control. Your outgoing flamboyant personality often hides the pain and turmoil that stems from your childhood. Sexual abuse is often the cause of this condition, however not in all cases. If you didn't experience sexual abuse in your own life then it may be related to ancestral trauma that has been triggered in your life.

Crying discussed in Volume 1.

See Anxiety, Colic, Depression

Cumulative Trauma Disorder (also known as Repetitive Stress Injury, RSI)

See Back Problems, Inflammation, Joint Problems, Muscle Problems, Myofascial Pain Syndrome (MPS), Rotator Cuff Problems, Tendon Problems

Emotions

This condition often arises when you are participating in an activity during which you may be feeling negative emotions such as anger, resentment, rage or irritation. You may be feeling overly sensitive, because you've been on the receiving end of critical judgment, verbal abuse or punishment. You often punish yourself, as you were not allowed to show signs of anger during childhood. Only authority figures were allowed to vent their anger—you were punished for expressing frustration or anger.

Cut

See Accident, Bleeding, Blood Problems

Emotions

You feel angry and are holding onto old grudges. What happened or how did you feel emotionally (or even a thought that was upsetting or angered you) before you cut yourself? You are trying to dissociate from what is happening in your life. What are you unhappy about? Explore any recent circumstances. Which part of the body was injured? See the Quick Reference Guide for more information that is related to the injured body part.

Cushing's Disease

See Adrenals, Grave Disease, Pituitary Gland Problems

Emotions

You may be exhausted from always being emotionally available to everyone. There is a need to break away from unhealthy and destructive patterns. These patterns include internal conflict, destructive thoughts coming to the surface and sabotaging your goals. You may have experienced a significant trauma during childhood that influenced your hormone levels, leaving you in survival and stress mode for long periods of time. You also experienced stress during womb stages where your mother's stress levels were heightened, possibly placing stress on you during developmental stages.

Cystic Fibrosis

See Cyst, Digestive Problems, Inflammation, Liver Problems, Lung Problems, Sinus Problems,

Emotions

There is always urgency when achieving or accomplishing goals, as you fear you will fail or that opportunities might pass you by if you don't act quickly enough. Stressful circumstances have left you feeling out of control and unable to get back on track and reconnect with what you once loved doing in life. This may be as a result of paying more attention to the needs of others rather than you own. This has left you feeling empty, unfulfilled or resentful.

Lungs: See the Lung section in the book. Your suppressed grief, lack of passion for life and fear of failure may have gotten the better of you. You seem to feel unclear about how you can achieve your goals and have your needs met at the same time.

Digestive system: See Digestive Problems. This area in the body relates to feeling conflicted with the environment and personal relationships. There is a lack of understanding between you and family members. It is causing you a great deal of stress, making everything feel toxic and dangerous.

Cyst

See Abscess, Breast Cyst, Cancer, Endometriosis, Hormone Problems, Polycystic Ovary Syndrome, Sebaceous Cyst

Emotions

You seem to feel misunderstood by influential people, which cause you to feel alone and empty. You may be feeling a great deal of sadness, grief and lack sufficient support in your life. You may be feeling a great deal of resentment as a result of past traumas and injustices. You seem to feel stuck and stagnant with emotional baggage, which has become a suit of armor that you use to protect yourself from experiencing old trauma again. You may feel that you are your own best friend, finding comfort in being alone.

Discussed in Volume 1: Cysts on the head, Cysts on the neck, Cysts on the back, Cysts on arms, Cysts on upper body / chest / stomach, Cysts on legs

Cystitis

See Bacteria, Bladder Problems, Bladder Cancer, E.coli, Inflammation / Infection

Emotions

You feel guilty whenever you express any emotional needs. You feel that you don't deserve to have your needs met. Your expression for love is often met with punishment and rejection. You have been regularly reminded that you have to work hard for what you want in life. Goals are not easily achieved. You often feel that you have to hold yourself back so that others can accelerate in life. This often stems from a childhood where you were not supported in your goals and the needs of others always came first. Your goals felt like pipedreams.

Dandruff

See Hair Problems, Skin Problems

Emotions

This condition often relates to current responsibilities that are causing you to feel stressed. You may be feeling vulnerable as your plan of action (for goals, work, family etc.) may have a crack in it. Re-evaluate the structure of your plans and whether the people supporting you are for your highest and best. You need to find a better balance between your goals and your colleagues' / loved ones' goals as there seems to be conflict. Find a balance between your role and the roles of those people who are supporting you.

Deafness

See Acoustic Neuroma, Hearing Impairment, Nerve Problems

Degenerative Joint Disease

See Arthritis, Inflammation, Joint Problems, Osteoarthritis, Osteoarthritis, Tendon Problems

Delirium

See Hysteria, Schizophrenia

Emotions

You are experiencing outbursts of powerful emotions that were suppressed by your parents and ancestors. Strong emotions may have been felt and suppressed between your mother and father during your conception and these emotions may have been triggered in your life. The emotions may have built-up to a point where you feel unable to control them. The outbursts come in waves. Emotional bursts are like a crashing wave, then everything subsides, while the wave (emotion) is drawing back into the ocean, until the next set of waves comes crashing down.

Delirium Tremens

See Addictions, Alcoholism, Hysteria

Emotions

You are suffering from alcohol withdrawal. You may be feeling lost without a quick fix and there is nothing to reach out to for comfort. Alcohol was your crutch and helped you to suppress negative emotions. The trustworthy source of comfort (alcohol) is not readily available anymore and you are going into a panic. This is almost the same as not getting attention, safety, nurturing or comfort from your mother. You may have had a mother that was hostile towards you.

Dementia

See Hysteria, Multiple Personality Disorder, Senility

Emotions

You refuse to accept the world as it is and want to rebel against the fact that it is restrictive and controlling. You feel stuck and stagnant in life due to a childhood that made you feel hopeless and disempowered. Your mother and father behaved in a way that caused you to feel out of control and helpless. There was no proper guidance and support available to you. You often feel scattered and incoherent, as there was nothing or no one to hold on to and reach out to when you experienced trauma. You feel weak and disempowered when you need to fight your battles.

Demyelinating Disease

See Multiple Sclerosis

Dengue

See Fever, Parasites, Rash, Skin Problems, Virus

Emotions

You feel that people's words and actions are affecting and influencing you skin deep. You may feel utterly unworthy of expressing your emotions. You seem to be punishing yourself for feeling hostile and negative emotions as you were taught that such emotions are bad and not allowed. This type of pattern caused you to suppress your boundaries and self-worth. You feel that you have to work hard to be seen, appreciated and acknowledged.

Depression

See Adjust Disorder, Anxiety, Hyper-Somnia, Nervous Breakdown, Panic Attack, Post-Traumatic Stress Disorder (PTSD), Seasonal Adjustment Disorder (SAD)

Emotions

You seem to feel hopeless and useless, misunderstood by the people around you. It feels like you've have been kicked out of the community circle and you feel devalued. You are struggling with internalized anger and may find that existing infections in your body (often intestines) can flare up quickly due to the anger that is always lurking in the unconscious mind. You can secretly be very judgmental about other people's lives, projecting your bitterness about what was missing in your life. You may project a façade that is the opposite of being depressed. You want to hide how you feel, as you do not want others to see your feelings of shame and guilt. You feel as if no one is allowed to see you for who you are. You may feel that people only notice you when you behave a certain way.

Dermatitis

See Eczema, Itching, Rashes, Skin Problems

Emotions

This condition is often brought on by stress that could be work or family related. You may feel overly responsible for the tasks or burdens of others. You are often in a role where people rely on you too much. You are often part of a family where members may emotionally rely on you. You feel that you have to be the foundation for others to lean on because if you don't do it, no one else will.You often accept extra responsibilities as the acknowledgement and praise that follow is emotionally rewarding and fulfilling—you take pride in being someone other's put their trust in. Working hard means that you can avoid being on the receiving end of insults, being ridiculed, or attacked (either verbally or physically). Your role means that others rely on you instead of seeing you as target or threat. People may take advantage of your giving nature; your poor boundaries cause you to feel invaded, powerless or taken advantage of. You may begin to feel increasingly unhappy with life and even resentful as a result of the position that you are in.

Discussed in Volume 1: Another form of Dermatitis is Pompholyx.

Diabetes

See Carpal Tunnel Syndrome, Eye Problems, Hypoglycemia, Nerve Problems, Pancreas Problems

Emotions

Many people have reported that stress was the main issue in their life when they were diagnosed with diabetes. They also reported that the stress was due to feeling out of control, fighting against someone or circumstances that caused them to experience great stress. This also includes being overwhelmed with responsibility and having a lack of control over certain people and circumstances. Often there is a trauma related to the death of a loved one that has never been processed. You may have an unmet need for love and nurturing and feel that if you accept responsibilities on behalf of others, you will receive love (work for love). You seem to feel unfulfilled with what you have accomplished in life, realizing that you may have missed out on your life's purpose because you were distracted by a fear of success.

Diarrhea

See Bacteria, Digestive System, Diverticulitis, Intestines, Virus

Emotions

You often feel conflicted between your emotions and what you see in your environment. You do not want to let go of your problems. You do not feel safe and secure and often suffered regular rejection from a parent or other influential people. You are trying to rid yourself of abusive patterns, negative people and unhealthy relationships in an internal, violent way. Physically the body could be responding to an infection which means that you are irritated and angry with someone or a situation in your life that you want to (but can't) escape. This could also be a long-standing issue that has taken a toll on you, affecting your immune system. This has caused you to be more vulnerable to infections in the intestine.

Digestive Problems

See Anal Problems, Bloated, Cancer, Colon Cancer, Colon Problems, Constipation, Hypophosphatemia, Intestine Problems, Irritable Bowel Syndrome, Liver, Nausea, Prolapsed Bowel, Stomach, Ulcers, Vomit

Emotions

Issues in this area can arise due a fear of "digesting or stomaching" a current situation or past circumstances. It may also be a refusal or stubbornness to accept what's happening in reality. You may feel that your ability to feel empowered has been suppressed; therefore you have reverted to stubbornness as a substitute for the loss of power in life. You often feel emotionally inflexible when adjusting to new routines, plans or changes. You are critical of yourself and are unforgiving of your own mistakes.

Diverticulitis

See Colon Problems, Diarrhea, Digestive Problems, Intestines

Emotions

You seem to be reliving past experiences and are only processing small amounts of your trauma while suppressing the rest. You are very self-conscious of your appearance and how others see you. You feel held back in life, almost as if you are not allowed to have fun and enjoy the good things. You seem to sabotage anything good that comes into your life. You are fearful of accepting love and allowing yourself to feel loved as it may leave you exposed and open to attack. You may have made a negative association with love and nurturing.

Dizziness

See Circulation Problems, Concussion, Headache, Nerve Problems, Vertigo

Emotions

Dizziness is often related to self-sabotage as it stops a person from doing certain things that they do not like to do. You might be feeling guilty about doing something instead of setting time aside for yourself. You might be unconsciously distracting yourself from making personal progress. You feel conflicted with your current circumstances and are dissociating from what is going on. There has been a disruption of the flow of love and support in your life. This may be related to an argument you had with someone or you may be avoiding a situation that might provoke confrontation.

Down Syndrome

See Congenital Disorders

Dried Eyes

See Eye Problems – Dried Eyes

Duchenne Muscular Dystrophy

See Cramps, Kennedy's Disease, Muscle Problems, Myofascial Pain Syndrome (MPS), Motor Neuron Disease, Toxins, Tremor

Emotions

This is relevant to the parent that had the dystrophin gene[1]: You may have experienced a great deal of inner suppressed conflict during your child's conception. There may have been a battle between the sexes; perhaps a power struggle over control. Your mother may have been made to feel insignificant and unimportant. Figuratively speaking, her voice was not allowed to be heard and she were not allowed to be included in the decision making process. This role was for the dominant figure in the house (in some cases this could actually be the woman, which would then reverse the above mentioned roles).

---

[1] http: / / en.wikipedia.org / wiki / Duchenne_muscular_dystrophy

Dumping Syndrome

See Bloated, Digestive Problems, Nausea, Weight Problems

Emotions

Depression seems to accompany this condition, but bear in mind that the depression is often a secondary condition and not the cause. You feel that the bad and negative patterns in your life will not end, no matter how hard you try to stop or resolve them. You may feel that you are destined to suffer and be unhappy for the rest of your life. There is deep rage and anger that is suppressed due to fear of self-expression. This stems from an abusive and manipulative household (physically or emotionally) where you were afraid of your source of food (which would be the parents) from an early age.

Dupuytren's Contracture

See Fingers, Muscle Problems, Myofascia

Emotions

There seems to be unresolved trauma related to your childhood. You were unable to hold on to your mother during a stressful time or when you felt threatened by circumstances. Often your mother was emotionally absent as a result of her stressful circumstances. You felt that no one was paying attention or looking out for you.

Dyslexia

See Eye Problems, Learning Disability

Emotions

You seem to feel pushed and forced to accomplish and perform certain tasks. You feel unsupported and lack the guidance of influential people. The left and right hemisphere of your brain does not connect in harmony. You seem to be unable to decide who and what you want to be, including which gender you should be. A parent may have felt this way while you were still in the womb.

Dyspareunia (Painful Sex)

See Inflammation, Candida, Female Problems, Pain

Emotions

You seem to be feeling shame and guilt when you have sexual needs or are being intimate. You have been taught that sex is dirty. Your family may have had strong judgment and opinions about sex and sexuality. The message about sex was negative, which may have left you feeling, "It is wrong." You may feel that you are not allowed to take pleasure in sex and that it's a one sided activity where you have to attend to the other person's needs. You seem to have a fear of intimacy and may not feel comfortable with your partner, which causes you to emotionally dissociate whenever you are with this person. You may feel obligated to be with someone, which means that your heart and body are not willingly available to a partner. You might have feelings for someone else or feel that you are with the wrong partner.

Dystonia discussed in Volume 1.

See Cramps, Muscle Problems, Myofascial Pain Syndrome (MPS), Nerve Problems, Tic, Tremor

Eclampsia

See Female Problems, Hypertension, Hysterectomy, Pregnancy, Seizures

Emotions

Your relationship with your mother has left you feeling vulnerable, raw and rejected. There seems to be a deep unconscious fear that you may end-up being the same mother as she was. You know how much emptiness and pain your past has left you with and you do not want to recreate similar circumstances with your own child. You may fear that you cannot change the outcome of your relationship with your future child, the only tools you have are what you learned from your mother.

E.Coli

See Bacteria, Bloated, Digestive Problems, Intestines, Stomach Problems

Emotions

You may be feeling angry and resentful toward the self-sabotaging behavior of influential people who are holding you back. You feel that you're not allowed to do what you want, causing you to feel guilty for not living out your life's purpose. You regret not taking action when you should have in past circumstances. You are now unconsciously repeating influential people's self-sabotaging patterns and it's slowing down your personal progress.

Eczema

See Dermatitis, Inflammation, Itching, Rashes, Skin Problems

Emotions

You seem to feel controlled, judged or manipulated. You feel aggravated by those around you, as you realize that certain people are unhealthy to be around. You are too scared to move away from these people. You have a fear of losing your identity if these people aren't in your life. It may be a destructive environment but it feels familiar. You often feel bullied and held back by influential people in your life. You may have learned that you are not allowed to challenge those who are more powerful than you are. You often revert back to a victim state whenever you feel dominated or challenged. When you feel like a victim, you do not pose to be a threat anyone and avoid further attack.

Edema

See Allergies, Alcoholism, Cirrhosis, Heart Problems, Kidney Problems, Liver Problems

Emotions

You may feel under attack (either verbally or physically) by influential people that were supposed to love you. You don't feel safe receiving love and feel that it should be avoided and rejected at all cost. You are holding onto pain from the past as a reminder that others may hurt you if you allow yourself to be vulnerable and open to love. Love is toxic. You often feel responsible for the way you were treated in the past. You took on many responsibilities to overcompensate for feeling rejected and in the way.

Elbow Problems

See Joint Problems, Pain Tennis Elbow

Emotions

Elbow problems are related to feeling very indecisive. Not knowing whether to leave or continue a project, job or relationship. Feeling obligated to see things through however there is no benefit in doing so for you. Your loyalty and devotion to a project or person is holding you back. You don't necessarily need to move away from current circumstances however; you do need to change how you feel about it. You are growing and moving into a different direction in your life. Current circumstances may not be fulfilling enough to support the new changes that need to take place within yourself and your environment.

Elephantiasis

See Lymphatic Filariasis

Emphysema

See Addictions, Inflammation, Lung Problems, Pain, Smoking

Emotions

You seem to be feeling a great deal of guilt and regret due to past actions. You may have caused others a great deal of pain or stress and are afraid of being punished for making poor choices. You feel a great deal of stress, as you couldn't live up to the expectations of influential people. This results from a childhood where you may have been blamed for problems and stress in the family that was not your fault. You are unconsciously taking out your old hurt and pain on loved ones. There is a tendency to pull people into your depressed state so that others can see how deep the emotional wounds are. You often feel that others will never be able to understand to what extent you've had to endure stress.

Encephalitis

See Inflammation, Meningitis

Endometriosis

See Bleeding, Blood Problems, Cyst, Fallopian Tube Problems, Polyps, Uterus Problems

Emotions

You have suppressed your creativity and passion in life. You might have a fear of having children, as your own childhood experiences may have been traumatic. You have a fear your childhood history will repeat itself. You may also be attached to your independence, as this is where you feel most powerful. Bearing a child might challenge your ability to be independent of others. You might feel that being dependent on others will inevitably invite circumstances that will make you feel controlled and trapped. Your life has been consumed by responsibilities, a lack of guidance and having to fend for yourself. You need a break from this strenuous and challenging cycle. You seem to feel quite resentful of being a female, always pulling the short end of the rope in society. You have seen women being treated unfairly, abused or disrespected, causing you to try and avoid experiencing the same treatment.

Epilepsy

See Catalepsy, Hysteria, Nerve Problems, Pineal Gland Problems, Seizures, Schizophrenia
Emotions
You have piled all of your emotions into one bag and that bag is now overflowing. The more emotions you suppress, the more explosive the outpour of emotions are when provoked. You may have been pushed too hard during childhood; there was no room for error. You are painfully sensitive to criticism; the slightest disagreements strike you in the heart, leaving you upset, angry or resentful. You have become overly sensitive to criticism and may even lash out as a result of frustration and not having a clear discernment about how you should communicate personal boundaries. If you start to accept / believe the regular criticism of others, you often become you own worst critic.

Esophagus

See Muscle Problems, Throat Problems
Emotions
You seem to find it challenging to digest and process your reality. You thought you were living a good life, until unexpected changes took place that began to alter the picture perfect reality. You find yourself in the unsatisfactory position of having gained and lost something at the same time. You are not sure what to make of these changing circumstances. You may have deep-seated secrets / emotions that are being triggered however you do not have anyone you trust to confide in. Your suppressed emotions are often accompanied with denial and a refusal to see that there is a problem that needs to be addressed.

Estrogen / Oestrogen

See Depression, Hot Flushes, Fallopian Tube Problems, Female Problems, Hysterectomy, Menopause, Ovary Problems, Pregnancy, Weight Problems
Emotions
You may feel uncomfortable in your own skin. You are not sure what is expected of you as a female or male in your environment. You have had a challenging or confusing relationship with your mother or other influential female figure(s). In your opinion, feminine figures, or being feminine is perceived as being weak and more prone to being attacked or used by people. You may have witnessed women or people's femininity being demeaned and disregarded, which may have left you questioning your own value as an individual. How and when you project your feminine qualities may have been controlled by your environment, influential people around you and childhood circumstances.

Eye Problems

See Astigmatism, Blindness, Bloodshot Eyes, Cataracts, Conjunctivitis, Diabetes, Far-Sighted, Macula, Maxillary Sinus, Myasthenia Gravis, Muscle Problems, Near-Sighted, Paget's Disease, Pinguecula, Pink Eye, Pterigium, Retina
Emotions
Eyesight can be challenged by pregnancy and diabetes. People with eye problems often find it challenging to accept support from others. You are often rigid about certain aspects of your life that you do not want to consciously become aware of, whether it is an abusive family

history or current issues. This could include a failing marriage as well as not wanting to be seen by others. The more stress, anxiety and abuse you have experienced, the more contracted and rigid the muscles behind the eyes become, resulting in bad eyesight. This rigidity could also be related to an ancestry where people had to be emotionally hard and rigid in order to survive challenging times. You often lose sight of what you want in life and how you are going to attract it. Sometimes you need to be pushed or rescued from your own destructive circumstances. As a result of a stressful and even abusive childhood, you tolerate being abused or punished by others. Stressful and abusive circumstances have become a way of life. You feel comfortable with being uncomfortable.

Failed Back Syndrome (Post-Laminectomy Syndrome)

See Back Problems, Pain

Emotions

You may feel that life has failed you. Your physical body is caving in from all the responsibilities you are holding on to. You seem to be feeling responsible for everything and everyone else's happiness and health, while you put your emotional and physical needs last. You may have been taught to serve and always look after other people's needs before attending to your own. People may not always have appreciated your efforts and strain you went through to support and help others.

Fallopian Tube Problems

See Birth, Cancer, Cyst, Estrogen Problems, Female Problems, Hysterectomy, Miscarriage, Ovary Problems, Pregnancy

Emotions

You feel a great deal of anger and frustration when developing new ideas that would compliment your creativity. What you want is within reach. You think too far ahead causing yourself to sabotage your present life and goals. Often your creativity and passion is accompanied with frustration and stress, as a direct result of feeling pressured and controlled by a dominant figure. You felt that all your goals were controlled by influential people's hidden agendas. You may feel that you have no choice other than to abandon your goals and fulfill the expectations of others. Your dreams and goals always come at a price and that price is often related to time and support, which you seem to lack.

Fatigue (includes Chronic Fatigue Syndrome)

See Adrenal Problems, Fibromyalgia, Hypothalamus, Leaking Heart Valve, Lupus, Malaria, Menstrual Problems, Pineal Gland Problems, Scurvy, Sleep Disorders, Tremor

Emotions

General Overview

There are a few factors, which might help to understand who develops CFS (out of the many with stress and trauma). One simple factor is physical exhaustion and depletion. People suffering from CFS spent a great deal of their life feeling like they had to be on guard. It is almost as if there is a danger in their life which they cannot identify. Their adrenals worked over-time, holding them in a constant state of fight or flight. The body can only withstand this behavior for a certain amount of time. In this case, CFS is a symptom of the body's depleted ability to respond to the constant sense of threat. The body is often stuck in survival mode, without the resources to maintain this state. Any energy that the body creates is immediately used by the body's survival system, meaning the benefit from rest is very short-lived. You feel overwhelmed with life and need a way out. You are still holding on to and investing energy into disappointments. Your resentment serves to remind you that unresolved injustices would need to be corrected one day. You may feel disappointed with yourself as a result of missed opportunities. You do not want to face certain circumstances in your life anymore. The fatigue unconsciously gives you an alternative option to keeping trauma from surfacing.

Female Problems discussed in Volume 1.

See Abortion, Birth, Estrogen Problems, Eclampsia, Fallopian Tube Problems, Hysterectomy, Mid Life Crisis, Miscarriage, Ovary Problems, Pregnancy, Uterus Problems

Fetal Alcohol Syndrome

See Alcoholism, Birth / Womb

Emotions

Child suffering from FAS: The associations that you made with your mother often starts at implantation. Anger, resentment, lack of empathy, violence, rage, hostility, poisoning, toxicity (alcohol and other substances) or feeling attacked (either verbally or physically) may have been present during the conception stages. This may leave the child in an emotional state, creating many future problems for the child and parent. You often rebel against authority and anyone that challenges your free will.

Fever

See Coxsackie, Inflammation, Malaria, Meningitis, Mercury Poisoning, Lupus Pneumonia, Scarlet Fever, Septicemia, Serum Sickness, Toxins, Virus

Emotions

You are stuck in a situation in which you have had enough. It has caused you to feel blocked in many areas of your life. Your frustration and exhaustion has now physically surfaced. You are trying to rid yourself of an unhealthy lifestyle, working patterns, friendships or criticism and controlling individuals or unnecessary responsibilities. You may have overwhelmed your system with the strong emotions you are feeling. You are trying to rid your life of toxic relationships and people who cause you to feel unsafe and under attack.

Fibroids

See Uterine Fibroid

Fibromyalgia

See Accident, Asthma, Chronic Fatigue Syndrome, Cramps, Gulf War Syndrome, Hyper-Somnia, Inflammation, Muscles Problems, Tendon Problems

Emotions

FM might be a secondary symptom of a different condition that started first. My suspicion is that it could be a secondary symptom of infections, car accidents, traumatic childbirth or even chemical exposure. Muscles resonate with the emotions of having to be right, control issues, ego, guilt and stubbornness. You may not want to let go of certain circumstances and injustices in your life that are aggravating the FM. You fear that if you let go of your unhealthy habits then you might lose people in your life that resonate with you. What you may not be aware of is that you often resonate with and are attracted to people who share the same self-sabotaging and unhealthy patterns.

Fingers

See Arthritis, Dupuytren's Contracture, Joint Problems, Inflammation, Muscles Problems, Nail Biting, Tendon Problems

You may feel unprotected and lack enough resources and support in order to move forward in life feeling safe. You may have been the buffer between family members, copping the consequences of confrontation as a result. You don't believe in your own ability to be successful without the support of selfish / emotionally unavailable influential people. It is time for you to stop waiting for the approval or permission of someone to make progress in your life and to take action on your goals.

Flesh Eating Disease

See Necrotizing Fasciitis

Flu

See Congestion, Fever, Sinus
Emotions
You are feeling under the weather and also under someone's thumb. You may be feeling trapped and controlled in your life, as if your sacred space is violated. Your need for a change and a bit of freedom with less responsibilities has become more desirable. You may have developed the flu to give a valid reason to make time for yourself without feeling guilty. You may have been focusing on the future too much. Your overwhelming fear of the unknown future may have caused you a great deal of stress. You feel resistant to change and are afraid of the consequences theses changes may bring.

Food Poisoning

See Poisoning

Foot Problems (includes Ankles)

See Back Problems, Bone Problems, Bursitis, Hip Problems, Knee Problems, Neck Problems, Pelvic Problems, Plantar Fasciitis, Skeletal System, Spine Problems, Tendon, Toes
Emotions
People use this part of their body to physically and emotionally move forward. If there are issues with the feet then it's a clear indication that the person often fears consequences related to change. This is related to moving forward, reaching success, commitment or a fear of losing control. You may have had a shortage of guidance and support in the past when going through different stages. You fear losing control of your destiny and the outcome of any new changes you manifest.

Frost Bite

See Blood, Skin Problems

Emotions

You may be feeling very challenged by your self-sabotaging patterns as you feel unable to break unhealthy patterns. This self-sabotaging pattern has kept you out of the spotlight. You seem to overcompensate for the lack of acknowledgement you received during childhood, by often keeping yourself small. You have learned that when you put yourself out in the world, you are vulnerable to attack.

Frozen Shoulder

See Accidents, Back Problems, Cramps, Muscle Problems, Myofascial Pain Syndrome (MPS), Shoulder Problems

Emotions

Frozen shoulder may be the result of fearing being out of control. You feel a great deal of regret over bad decisions that influenced the quality of life for you and your family. This may have included the loss of a job, a failed marriage or missed opportunities. You may also be going through a phase where you don't feel as empowered, powerful, respected or admired anymore. This could be related to menopause, mid-life crisis, change of jobs or a failed marriage. You may feel stuck between two romantic partners or have a desire to be with someone else. However, due to obligations to the family, you stick around. The key here is to find what out happened when the frozen shoulder started. What emotions were present and how did those emotions make you feel?

Fungus

See Candida, Intestines, Rash, Skin Problems

Emotions

You are holding on to trauma that you can't let go of. You often feel that someone has to pay and take responsibility for the pain and injustice that was inflicted upon you. Your resentment has become more than a familiar old feeling—it is almost a part of you and you don't know who you are without your feelings of betrayal, injustice or disappointment.

Gall Bladder

See Digestive Problems, Liver Problems

Emotions

You feel very challenged when faced with harsh relationships. This is often related to the harshness of a father figure. You are a timid and gentle person who feels a great need to overcorrect personal boundaries. This is a result of feeling taken advantage of in the past and a fear of establishing clear boundaries.

Gall Stones

See Gall Bladder, Inflammation,

Emotions

Bitterness and resentment seems to be main key issues here. Past trauma and pain cannot be pushed aside anymore. The need for vengeance, an apology and justice are blocking you from moving forward. You analyze your emotions instead of feeling them in the heart mind. This method has served you well until now.

Gangrene discussed in Volume 1.

See Accident, Bacteria, Blood, Diabetes, Inflammation

Gas

See Allergies, Colon Problems, Cramps, Digestive Problems

Emotions

You are holding on to old fears and trauma that is triggered by your current lifestyle. You struggle with interpreting these feelings and end up holding onto the emotions. You desperately need to enforce boundaries, as others have not respected your personal space.

Genital Warts

See Immune System, Virus

Emotions

You feel ashamed and disgusting for having sexual needs. Your sexual needs and feelings are in conflict with the family values and beliefs. The sex topic was only meant for adults in your family because children have no business understanding what is going on in the adult world, as it was too disgusting and shameful to talk about. As a result, the parent(s) projected their guilt and shame toward sexuality onto you.

Gingivitis

See Gum Problems

Goiter

See Cancer, Graves's Disease, Hashimoto's, Hypothyroidism, Inflammation, Immune System, Pituitary Problems

Emotions

Your truth has become a heavy burden to suppress. No one is listening but what you need to say is becoming an urgent matter. You always seem to wait for the right moment to speak, however that moment never takes place. You often hold onto angry words. As a result of long-term suppression and being overly controlled by influential people, you refrain from speaking up. You seem to need permission to move beyond rules that have been laid out for you by influential people.

Gonad Problems

See Female Problems, Infertility, Male Problems, Ovary Problems, Penis Problems, Prostate Problems, Testosterone Problems

Gonorrhea

See Bacteria, Female Problems, Male Problems, Pelvic Problems

Emotions

You do not respect your body, your sexuality or gender. This may be as a result of being treated in a way that reinforced your vulnerable low self-esteem. You seem to have been in a family where there was a lack of respect, support, compassion or love. Hostility, coldness and unpredictable moods often dominated the household. You may have been manipulated with shame and made to feel guilty for who and what you are.

Gout

See Arthritis, Joint Problems, Pain

Emotions

People affected by gout often have very strong control issues. You may feel immensely out of control and disempowered. This is a result of not being able to exercise healthy boundaries during childhood. You are overcompensating for the lack of control in your life by being overly controlling. When you need to be in control, you often exhibit a passive-aggressive streak. This passive-aggressive pattern has now come to a halt, as your emotions are now turning into simmering rage.

Granulopenia

See Attack, Blood Problems, Immune System

Graves Disease

See Goiter, Hashimoto's, Hyperthyroidism, Thyroid Problems

Emotions

You feel angered by what you are seeing in your life and environment. Your anger and powerlessness have transformed into frustration. You have made the association that expression = punishment, abuse, criticism or abandonment. You are desperate to say what needs to be said and will take a verbal blow if necessary. After the consequences of speaking up have subsided, you are still left reeling with anger, as you were unable to have the last word and completely express yourself. There is a great deal of unresolved trauma; leaving you to stew over what has been said and done. You feel angry over what should have been said and done instead of what the initial outcome was.

Gulf War Syndrome

See Attack, Chronic Fatigue, Diarrhea, Fibromyalgia, Lung Problems, Nerve Problems, Post-Traumatic Stress Disorder (PTSD), Radiation, Rashes, Skin Problems, Suicide, Toxins

Emotions

You feel overpowered, invaded, controlled or attacked (either verbally or physically). You feel resentful, as you were not able to protect yourself or loved ones against challenging or threatening circumstances. This has left you feeling powerless, anxious, numb or frozen. You blame authorities for the injustices that you have had to experience. You feel a great deal of anger toward influential people who controlled the destiny of those who needed protection and security. This caused you to doubt and not trust others. You feel, "No one is looking after my interests," with a sense that you have a bleak future ahead. Your reality has been torn apart and you find it challenging to trust others.

Gum Problems

See Anxiety, Bacteria, Bleeding, Scurvy

Emotions

Anger and resentment related to making a decision and expressing yourself seems to be the main focus. This may be as a result of feeling suppressed or threatened by an influential person or partner. You can't decide how you should feel about your life, circumstances and the people that are part of it. You feel unable to make decisions because you are indecisive and feel frustrated about what to do. You may also have a partner that is more dominant with the decision making process.

Gingivitis (Bleeding gums)

You seem to feel angry in regards to what you can or cannot say. You regret not saying what needed to be said in the past, as you know it would have changed the outcome of stressful circumstances that took place. When confronted, you feel challenged to communicate your self-worth and personal opinion.

Hands / Arms

See Dislocated Shoulder, Fingers, Humerus, Joint Problems, Muscle Problems, Shoulder Problems, Tendon Problems, Wrist Problems

Emotions

Right hand and Arm problems

Trouble reaching an agreement with someone as there may be a lack of trust. You may have a fear that the other person will not follow through on their agreement (fear of betrayal). You feel that you do not have the personal power or confidence to follow through on agreements you've made with others. You often find it challenging to commit to a project, a person or a goal. Commitment often = feeling controlled or trapped, with nowhere to hide. This triggers the running away instinct. You may feel conflicted when expressing a strong opinion you feel toward someone or your circumstances. This may be related to a prominent father figure who controlled your ability to make decisions. You have a fear of making a mistake in the eyes of your father.

Left hand and Arm problems

You may feel that you do not have enough personal power and confidence to execute a task. It begs the question, "Who challenged you when you accessed and exercised your talents?" You don't feel supported in your goals and projects. How did your mother behave when she executed tasks? Did she feel unworthy or not good enough and as a result, overcompensated by doing too much for others? Are you copying and expressing your mother or father's pattern? You do not nurture your spirituality, instead you feel dictated to and greatly influenced by the beliefs and values of others.

Hair Loss / Problems

See Aging, Alopecia, Anxiety, Depression, Mercury Poisoning, Tinea Capitis

Emotions

Hair loss is often a secondary symptom of a deeper medical issue. Hair loss can also be related to hormonal problems, cancer, long-term stress or malnutrition. It is also often linked to a person's connection to their spirituality and their relationship with their mother. Hair loss affects a person's ability to feel safe, to communicate and to feel good about their role in life. You may have experienced a relationship with an influential person who gave you very little room to make a mistake. This may have caused you to be too hard on yourself, perhaps even self-inflicting punishment if you feel you have not acted in a way that is pleasing to others.

Hansen's disease

See Leprosy

Hashimoto's

See Graves's Disease, Hypothyroidism, Inflammation

Emotions

You seem to have many self-sabotaging patterns that make you feel like you have to deprive yourself of the goodness in life. You may have experienced a childhood where guilt or abuse was used to control and manipulate you. You are in fear of making a mistake or doing something that could provoke an influential person, always trying too hard to avoid being punished. Dominant, controlling or influential people, such as a father or authority figure, have disempowered you.

Hay Fever

See Under Allergies / Pollen

Headaches

See Atlas Problems, Dizziness, Migraines, Muscle Problems, Nerve Problems, Sinus Problems

Emotions

The environment and circumstances are overwhelming. There are too many things you are trying to do and these activities do not resonate with your actual needs. You seem to get caught up in other people's stressful circumstances and don't always know when and where to draw the line. You find it difficult to shift the focus back to your own life. It does beg the question, "What will happen if you shift the focus back to you and become fully present?" You might choose to worry about others as this allows you to deflect your own problems.

Head Lice

See Parasites

Emotions

You often feel ashamed about yourself and exercise poor boundaries. You may feel used, abused, bullied or controlled by others. You have allowed others to take advantage of your goodwill and now seem to feel resentful about your current position and circumstances. This may be as a result of feeling disempowered and unable to stand your ground at this time. You feel fearful when you are in a situation that requires you to say "no" or stand up for yourself. Your confidence has been greatly challenged in the past.

Hearing Impairment

See Acoustic Neuroma, Ear Problems, Meniere's Disease, Nerve Problems, Tinnitus

Emotions

You feel frustrated with your surroundings and need to block it out. At the same time, this leaves you deeply conflicted with a desire to know the truth behind the circumstances. An influential person may have challenged your sharp nature. This authority figure may have suppressed you as he or she challenged your limitations (either mentally or emotionally or both). You may have been on the receiving end of criticism and judgment. This may have left you half broken and feeling as if the wounds are never going to heal. You do not feel understood; you also feel that others do not want to take the time to understand you. This causes you to feel unworthy and like a nuisance. You feel challenged by loneliness and emptiness; feeling unwanted by the rest of society. You often feel resentful and bitter as a result of unfair treatment you have had to endure.

Discussed in Volume 1: Born deaf, Left side problems, Right side problems, Ruptured ear drum, Water in ear.

Heart Problems

See Anxiety, Arrhythmia, Bleeding, Cardio-Vascular Problems, Circulation Problems, Hypertension, Hypoxia, Muscle Problems, Myofascial Pain Syndrome (MPS), Panic Attack

Emotions

Clients have reported that they also struggle with kidney and thyroid issues along with their heart problems. This association makes a lot of sense. When the heart is not expressing feelings and emotions, the kidneys and thyroid can suffer due to the back up caused by the lack of expression, regret, resentment and of control. You may not feel safe expressing emotions or don't feel worthy of being paid attention to. Some people say that the connection to the heart is the connection to the world. Once that connection has been disrupted, it influences one's judgment, of yourself and others. People love and feel from their heart (unless there is trauma relating to this area). When they have experienced trauma that caused a disruption in the heart mind they have difficulty with their relations. You will find it challenging to establish your identity, role or territory. You may feel very lonely and abandoned, as it can be difficult to identify and establish your uniqueness or safe haven. You only want to love and be loved. However, you have made a negative association with love during childhood. You may feel that love is hostile; love is dangerous, that receiving love only hurts or is traumatizing. The love you gave may have been used against you with abuse or you may have been made to feel like a nuisance. You have had to fight for your identity and personal space to be respected and acknowledged.

Heart Attack

Emotions

Heart attacks are often related to feeling challenged around the love topic (heart mind) and territory (home/personal space and role in the family). It also relates to a need to be in charge of your environment. Your ability to step into that role has been challenged by influential people or a partner. You are in conflict with those who are closest to you, feeling like you have to fight to be acknowledged, respected and validated. You put other's needs before your own, often having trouble finding the balance between meeting your needs and helping others. This can be especially difficult if you are the breadwinner of the family. This could also surface as the other extreme. You may be suffering from a lack of love and nurturing. As a result, you have become very controlling, demanding, competitive or selfish. You may feel that there is a great deal of scarcity in everything you need. You feel very challenged by low self-worth as you often felt you weren't good enough in childhood. You often blame, criticize and judge others as a result of venting your anger and frustration. You use the same emotional coping "tools" to communicate your truth to others. By projecting judgment towards others, you deflect from your own emotional tension, stress and burdens.

Heart By-Pass
Emotions
You have overwhelmed yourself as a result of your need to be in control of everything. Your control issues have been triggered by your family lifestyle in which there was no order, respect or sufficient support. You had to keep it all together as no else could or would. Your childhood foundation was built on feelings of mistrust, guilt or shame and you may have been made to feel incompetent.

Heart Murmur
Emotions
You may feel that you have to be low maintenance to those who show you affection. Being too needy or asking for too much may cause you to feel rejected or abandoned. The amount of love you receive is dependent on how much love you give. As a result, you give as much love as you can. Growing up, you felt belittled, often treated as though it was a privilege for you to be loved by influential people. This typically stems from a family where one parent had a loving nature and the other parent was abusive / distant or emotionally absent. It left you feeling confused as to what love and affection should be. The message and expression of love was scattered and inconsistent. Dissociation often follows when you do not understand or emotionally relate to the environment and expressed emotions.

Heart Overgrowth
Emotions
You felt overwhelmed by your mother's stress. There is a pattern of worrying too much about the welfare of others. This often stems from an ancestral pattern where a person felt overly responsible for others and concerned about the welfare of others. You often feel confused or unclear as to whom you can and should trust in life. You may have a history of allowing people to manipulate your integrity. You have bottled up emotions as you have a fear of expressing your emotions and desires as you will be seen as mentally and emotionally weak. You want to appear strong for the sake of others and to avoid potential humiliation. You dissociate from your emotions and this pattern has now physically caught up with you.

Heart Palpitations
Emotions
You do not feel at peace with yourself or the world around you. You seem to be stuck between two instincts, running and feeling frozen. You often expect the worst, which stems

from a parent who used drama to instill fear and manipulate by means of guilt and shame. Your adrenals are often exhausted and react to any given situation that feels remotely threatening by preparing the body to defend itself. You could have experienced a great deal of anxiety while in utero. You may have felt your mother's anxiety and stress after birth, the first time she held you. You formed a bond with her while she was in an anxious and exhausted state. You may have mimicked your mother's physical and emotional behavior during stressful circumstances, especially after birth.

Leaking Heart Valve
Emotions
You feel obligated to give love while expecting very little in return. When you do find the love you have been working and searching for, you are not allowed to embrace and accept it. This is as a result of your low self-esteem. You may have been made to feel guilty in the past for seeking attention, without earning it first. You often lack the stability of a healthy functioning family and feel that no one is reliable enough. You've experienced disappointment in the past as people failed you.

Multi Valve Heart Defect
Emotions
You have given too much of yourself and are now depleted. You may not have been able to practice clear boundaries as a child. You were taught to serve, protect, support and help others; often putting your own needs as last priority. You feel unsupported and unable to move forward with life due to a fear of failure. The reserved energy has been used to support everyone else's emotional or material needs. You feel conflicted about giving and receiving love, as this has always been bad news for you. You may feel guilty as you didn't love and support your nearest and dearest. This conflict and stubbornness is often the result of a tightly controlled childhood where you never knew what the mood in the house was going to be. No matter what you did, there was some sort of punishment awaiting you.

Heart Burn
See Acid Reflux, Nausea, Reflux, Rumination Syndrome
Emotions
You feel that you are always on the run and it is unsafe to be still. You feel overwhelmed by your upbringing, where negative and positive experiences always took place simultaneously. This only added to the pile of stress. You were taught to live and cope with a lack of love and support, as you would be punished if you asked for more than you were given. You were often made to feel guilty or ashamed whenever you expressed your needs.

Heat Stroke
See Cramps, Edema, Fever, Headache, Rashes
Emotions
You are pushing yourself too hard in an effort to show your determination to be successful in life. You have learned that the more you do for others, the more you are noticed, praised or loved. Because you take on so much, you often get yourself into circumstances where you need help. You are trying to care for too many people without considering the consequences.

You were pushed to work hard as a child and had to do things that did not resonate with you.

Heel / Heel Spurs

See Achilles Tendon Rupture, Bone Problems, Foot Problems, Inflammation, Pain, Plantar Fasciitis

Emotions

You are digging in your heels and have had enough of a recurring situation. This situation has moved from upsetting to causing irritation. You have the willingness to break your stubborn patterns however; you cling to it as it brings you a measure of safety. Your stubbornness has served you well and you have no intention of changing it. You may have learned to fight and fend for yourself and take pride in that. Your stubbornness and refusal to give in to others demands has helped you to move away from challenging circumstances. Like all bad habits and patterns, this takes a toll after a while and begins to surface physically.

Hemochromatosis

See Hormone Problems

Emotions

This is a genetic disease so you are almost certainly looking at family history and patterns. Scientific research suggests this condition is extremely widespread because it offered, at certain times, survival benefits or a competitive advantage. For example, during times of famine, when there was a lack of iron in the diet, people who retained too much iron would be more likely to survive and reproduce. The "success" of hemochromatosis is associated with strength and survival during times of hardship and adversity (especially nutritional challenges).

Hemorrhages

See Alcoholism, Anxiety, Bleeding, Depression, Diabetes, Hysteria

Emotions

Your circumstances left you stuck in a state of fear. You can't seem to find your place within the family and social life. You may feel that your fragile foundation (everything that your life has been built on) is beginning to cave in. You may feel controlled by an influential person and feel that you cannot break free from this person's controlling grip. You know this individual has a great deal of power over your life, causing you to feel intense anger and rage over the lack of control.

Hemorrhoids

See Anal Problems, Bleeding, Rectum Problems, Varicose Veins

Emotions

Your past has become such a part of your identity that you fear letting go of it, as part of you might die. "Who am I without my trauma, anxiety, anger, suffering or rejection?" You may be fearful of what others might think of you. You have a lot of self-doubt and trauma related to your failure to express yourself. You feel a great deal of shame related to your sexuality. You may have been humiliated as a result of your sexuality and the way in which you express yourself. You feel very controlled in everything that you do. You desperately want to escape your circumstances. As a result of being manipulated and controlled, you feel you have no bright future to look forward to.

Hepatitis

See Alcoholism, Blood Problems, Jaundice, Liver Problems, Virus

Emotions

You feel unworthy, ashamed, guilty or disgusting. You were made to feel less than worthy by those who needed to make you feel safe and protected. You often hold onto old unresolved anger from the past. You feel abused, manipulated or humiliated by loved ones. You felt abandoned, rejected or thrown away whenever you expressed boundaries within relationships and towards influential people. You deeply need to be loved, protected, nurtured and comforted. You often rely on others to make yourself feel safe and valued, as you cannot do this on your own.

Hernia

See Constipation, Digestive Problems, Intestines, Muscle Problems, Navel Problems, Pain, Rupture, Stomach Problems

Emotions

You often push people away, as you feel challenged whenever you need to express a boundary. You don't have to express clear boundaries when people are not around. You feel a great deal of stress and fear of rejection, when confronted with circumstances that would require you to express your needs. This may cause you to feel safer when pushing others away. In this way, you avoid being abandoned, rejected or manipulated by influential people. Love is not a safe topic for you because it seems to make you feel inadequate. This is especially true when push comes to shove and you have to show it, receive it, feel it or express it. You have made a negative association with love and as a result, you often push people away that are searching for love and acceptance from you. You may have been pushed away by your parents.

Herpes

See Spinal Cord, Virus

Emotions

You may not have felt valued, acknowledged or appreciated during childhood. You did not feel welcome in your own space and often felt like you were a nuisance. You are not comfortable in your own skin or in your relationships. Those feelings continue now and you feel misunderstood by your parents and those whose opinions you value. You may have a hostile relationship with your mother, as a result of misplaced trust. You may have learned to love your family out of fear. These were your only sources of love and you feared them. Your anger is a direct result of feeling powerless. You create arguments and confrontations with an unconscious intention of releasing suppressed fear, anger or resentment. You also recreate arguments that took place in your childhood that you have not processed or resolved. You often feel stuck and stagnant in your personal relationships. There is a communication barrier and it sabotages your ability to express your self-worth.

Hip Problems

See Arthritis, Bone Problems, Cancer, Cramps, Inflammation, Pelvic Problems
Emotions
You walk with anger and live with great frustration. You are suppressing a childhood trauma in which you had to watch your every step and action. You fear making decisions, as you do not know what the consequences will be or how influential people will respond. You do not trust your own judgment. You seem to feel in opposition with the people you want to reach out to for love and support. The most common pattern related to a hip problem is invasion trauma. It could either be related to emotional or physical issues. You may feel ashamed and are fighting to be respected in a controlling, suppressed or dominating environment. You are disappointed in your parents or caregivers for not meeting your needs in a way that made you feel valuable. You feel resentful for being part of a family where love was not easily shown. You may have been made to feel obligated to support others regardless of what your needs were at the time.
   Discussed in Volume 1: Hip Replacement, Ischium, Sacrum

Hives

See Allergies / Shellfish, Inflammation, Rashes, Skin Problems
Emotions
You feel irritated by your environment, family and relationships. You may have been made to feel painfully guilty for nothing. It could be that you've experienced intense fear and stress due an emotionally unpredictable, physically present but emotionally cold parent or family member. The tension between your mother and father was / is stressful for you. You often feel challenged by your family's behavior toward you. The bond with your mother may have been hostile. The way in which she met your emotional needs may not have necessarily been what you needed or longed for. This left you feeling emotionally unfulfilled in search of more validation, love or security; feeling abandoned and isolated.

Hormone Problems

See Estrogen Problems, Female Problems, Hyperthyroidism, Hypothyroidism, Male Problem, Pituitary Gland Problems, Testosterone Problems, Thyroid

Hot Flushes

See Estrogen Problems, Female Problems, Menopause, Pituitary Gland Problems, Prostate Cancer
Emotions
If you are young (teenager, mid twenties) then you may have been going through a very stressful time. Your body is in desperate need of a break as your emotions are causing stress on the body. You have been pushing yourself too hard and endured enough; your stress and anxiety has taken a toll on you mentally, emotionally, physically and spiritually. Hot flushes are often an expression of unspoken mixed emotions, especially anger. It is also related to not following your passion in life. Stepping into your life purpose is becoming an urgent matter. You feel held back by self-limitations such as doubt or of lack of confidence, as well as having no support.

Human Papillomavirus (HPV)

See Immune System Compromised, Virus

Emotions

You feel that you are not allowed to take control of your life. You may have given your power away to others, especially influential male figures. Being in the driver's seat was not tolerated during childhood. You observed one parent's submissive and disempowering reactions towards their partner. You may have made an association that emotional survival depends on giving your power away. You are expressing the submissive parent's unexpressed emotions either in the form of aggression, anger or a no-nonsense attitude. You often search for validation from a partner. Your mother or father (the opposite sex) did not meet your need for acknowledgement and acceptance.

Humerus

See Bone Problems, Elbow Problems, Hands / Arms, Muscle Problems

Emotions

You seem to feel unsure about whether you should proceed with an important decision or not. You may feel that the timing related to the start or end of a project is unclear. You feel that you do not have all the necessary facts / resources / knowledge or support to move into a specific desired direction or goal. There is deep fear of failure. You are afraid of the humiliation and consequences that might occur if you fail to meet goal(s). This is often related to childhood trauma when you intended to reach out to a person or object and were punished / smacked for doing so. "I can't have what I want."

Huntington's Disease

See Alzheimer's Disease, Kennedy's Disease, Multiple Personality Disorder (MPD), Tremor

Emotions

You have a great deal of compassion for the wellbeing of others (this also stems from your own need and yearning to be loved and treated with compassion). You tend to worry a lot and frequently become paranoid. You feel rigid and resistant to your constantly changing environment. Your first experience in life, such as birth and early childhood, may have been unpleasant or stressful. This may have caused you to become stubborn, angry or resistant in order to protect yourself from others who were seen as a potential threat.

Hyperglycemia

See Auto Immune System, Fatigue, Retina, Seizures, Skin Problems, Weight Problems

Emotions

You are depriving yourself of the goodness and sweetness life has to offer. You may have experienced punishment at times when you were happy. Now there seems to be an association that you do not deserve to have fun and enjoy the good things in life. You feel, "Fun and excitement is taboo for me, I am not allowed to see, feel or have any of it." You often battle against self-sabotaging patterns, which destroy any efforts to become successful. You feel that no matter how hard you work or how sincere your efforts are, you will end-up being overlooked and feeling inadequate.

Hyper-Somnia

See Depression, Chronic Fatigue, Fibromyalgia, Weight Problems

Emotions

You seem to be disconnecting from your environment. You feel overwhelmed by what is going on and feel obligated to take responsibility for other's actions. This may have caused you to experience a mentally, emotionally or spiritually draining past. Your current circumstances are triggering these unresolved issues that you have been trying to avoid. Your fatigue and mental dissociation served you during childhood and are still serving you now. This is often the result of not having opportunities to exercise clear boundaries—you've never felt safe saying "no."

Hypertension

See Anxiety, Arteries, Blood Pressure High, Circulation Problems, Heart Problems

Hyperthyroidism

See Goiter, Graves Disease, Inflammation, Menstrual Problems, Muscle Problems, Pituitary Gland Problems, Thyroid Problems

Emotions

You tried too hard to please others and are left feeling like a failure. Influential people did not acknowledge your efforts in a fulfilling way. You may have learned that achievement, success and very hard work will earn you the love that you are searching for. Love = work and exhaustion. You are placing a great deal of pressure on yourself to be better than before. You seem to spiral into a self-punishing cycle and panic when you cannot achieve goals or reach the expectations of others. Love in the family was very conditional. The influential people seemed to have been very success driven so any failures were stewed over and dwelled upon.

Hyperventilation

See Anxiety, Depression, Lactic Acidosis, Panic Attack

Emotions

A current issue has struck a very oversensitive cord in you. Circumstances or an individual in your life triggered an old traumatic ordeal. You do not know how to cope or process this long forgotten suppressed trauma. It is so overwhelming that it has left you gasping for air. You are painfully sensitive to judgment, critiques and the opinion of others. This is a result of a very low self-esteem and feeling unsupported during childhood. You have been under a great deal of pressure and stress. One incident may have triggered many pressing issues in your life.

Hypochondria

See Anxiety, Depression, Obsessive Compulsive Disorder

Emotions

You were exposed to a living environment where paranoia and over protection was dominant. Influential people may have projected fear onto you in order to gain control. Your mother and father may have found it challenging to keep their emotions, stress, tension and fears under wraps. You may have seen influential people fall victim to your own weaknesses and fears. As a child, you may have witnessed either a parent or caretaker spiraling out of control.

The parent may have become stuck in an emotionally silent, suppressed hysteria that is released when the tension becomes too intense.

Hypoglycemia

See Diabetes, Epilepsy

Emotions

You gave too much of yourself with the unconscious intention and desire of being acknowledged, loved and cared for in return. You have a hard time looking after your own needs. You may have experienced a situation that made you feel ashamed and guilty for putting yourself first. You come from a family where you may have been made to feel less worthy than others. You were made to feel ashamed for having needs when there were other matters that were more urgent. You had to be a part of circumstances that didn't resonate with you or give you any joy. Life was hard and very challenging in the ancestral line. There was no room for emotional or spiritual improvement, as there were always more urgent matters.

Hypophosphatasia

See Bone Problems, Digestive Problems, Miscarriage, Teeth Problems

Emotions

You may have experienced long-term challenges that caused you to feel too tense or traumatized. You couldn't digest and process emotions and incidents that took place in your environment. You may have experienced a pattern where everyone had to fend for himself or herself. Life has become too hard and strenuous. You feel that your body and spirituality are failing you. You seem to have made a traumatic association with nurturing and food (this is often an ancestral trauma). You may have consumed food in hostile and uncomfortable circumstances.

Hypotension

See Arteries, Blood Pressure Low, Heart Problems, Lactic Acidosis

Hypothalamus

Emotions

You seem to be storing a great deal of anger and feel restricted to express yourself. Suppressing your traumas is affecting your self-esteem, making you feel very insecure, anxious or overwhelmed. Other people's problems were always more important than your own. You have too many problems that have been thrown up in the air and you don't know which "tools" to use in order to deal with them all. This leaves you feeling scattered and these feelings begin to surface. You seem to feel utterly confused when it comes to what you need or want and you have a desire to give up. You often sabotage your goals, once you have moved out of your comfort zone. You are reluctant to accept help from others because you are afraid it will make you seem weak. You associate support with being controlled. You feel obligated to the people who support you and you energy stores are depleted.

Hypothyroidism

See Menstrual Problems, Muscle Problems, Pituitary Gland Problems, Thyroid Problems

Emotions

Pressure from outside influences pushed you to do more and accomplish more than others. In the case for those suffering from hypothyroidism, it had the opposite effect. You may have felt overwhelmed and strung out by too much pressure. You often felt that what was expected of you was out of reach. You'd rather give up than face failure and disappointment. You may not have had the support and love you needed in order to build your self-confidence. You felt that no one believed in you, as those close to you didn't acknowledge your good qualities.

Hypoxia

See Asbestosis, Blood Problems, Blood Pressure, Circulation Problems, Heart Problems, Liver Problems, Lung Problems, Necrosis

Emotions

You seem to feel as if you do not have enough of everything that you need in life. You may feel a lack of nurturing, protection, love or being cared for. You may feel that if your source of love, food and protection rejected you then the rest of the world will do the same. You feel, "What is the use of trying to make it in the world if this is how I am going to be treated?" Perhaps because you feel you will automatically be rejected anyway, you don't even take what life has to offer; you don't deserve it.

Hysterectomy

See Cyst, Estrogen Problems, Fallopian Tube Problems, Female Problems, Hot Flushes, Mid Life Crisis, Miscarriage, Ovary Problems, Uterus Problems

Emotions

You seem to feel as if you do not have what it takes anymore to be a successful and an independent feminine figure. You have suppressed the uniqueness of your femininity and may feel that it is unsafe to be a powerful female in society. You may have lived a life that revolved around catering to the needs of others. Inevitably, you have suppressed your passion and creativity to attend to people's needs. There is no passion and motivation behind your goals anymore. You have given so much to others, you find little to no source of love or energy left from which to draw passion, energy and creativity from.

Hysteria

See Catalepsy, Epilepsy, Nervous Breakdown, Panic Attack, Schizophrenia

Emotions

The past is haunting you to such an extent that you feel unable to run away from or escape it anymore (ancestral trauma). Ancestral trauma surfaced resulting in confusion as to what is your trauma and what is old, triggered ancestral trauma. You may feel that you have lost the battle with life and the challenges that have come your way. You have suppressed your stress and tension to a point where it has completely disempowered you. You feel as if all your demons are being released.

Icterus

See Jaundice

Ileitis

See Bacteria, Crohn's Disease, Digestive Problems, Intestine (Small Intestine) Problems, Virus

Emotions

You may feel very unworthy within your personal relationships. You are overly conscious of how family, friends and influential people see you, think of you and speak of and to you. You have transformed your identity into a façade that is pleasing to others and not necessarily pleasing to you. Being accepted is very important. You may have experienced a time when an influential person challenged your self-esteem, which caused you to feel inadequate and separate from the family. This may now cause you to back peddle out of situations that show signs of dominance and control. Dominating people in the past have burdened you emotionally.

Ilectomy

See Colon Problems, Inflammation

Immune System Compromised / Problems

See Alcoholism, Bacteria, Cancer, Lymphoma, Pineal Gland Problems, Poisons, Virus, Toxins

Emotions

When a person's immune system is compromised, the whole body suffers. You will be affected emotionally as well. When the immune system is compromised, problem areas in the body will often become worse as the immune system is not supporting problematic areas to heal. Along with unhealthy emotions, these problematic areas can become worse. You might feel that your support system has failed and you are challenged by your past. You are attracting new people and new circumstances into your current life that reinforce any childhood rejection. This includes abandonment trauma and feeling worthless and insignificant. You feel confused as to the intentions of others. You may have been through a whirlwind of emotional experiences that have left you feeling scattered, as well as emotionally and spiritually drained. You never know when to protect yourself or when to relax.

Impotence

See Aging, Gonad Problems, Male Problems, Mid Life Crisis, Penis Problems, Pituitary Gland Problems, Pineal Gland Problems, Sexual Abuse

Emotions

You feel shame and humiliation that is related to your sexuality. You feel fearful of past trauma that challenged your confidence and ability to feel safe during sex or with your sexuality. You may have come from a very conservative family, as though sex was a sacred act and not for pleasure. You may have been taught that any misuse of sex outside of marriage or recreation is disgusting and not allowed. Your parents used guilt and shame to bring this message across to you.

Incontinence

See Aging, Alcoholism, Bacteria, Inflammation, Female Problems, Male Problems, Muscle Problems, Myofascial Pain Syndrome (MPS), Male Problems, Urinary Infections

Emotions

Fear of an authority figure is the main key. You may be fearful of not being accepted by a strong dominant figure in your life. Your importance and value in life is based on this person's opinion of you. Explore what your mother's relationship was like with your father. Does she have a fear of him or a dominant figure in the family? You are internalizing your guilt and how you feel about yourself. As a result, you feel guilty for having such hostile emotions towards someone that you love out of fear. There could also be a deep ancestral fear of failing in the eyes of a male, father or dominant partner. This is often triggered by old ancestral trauma. There is a fear present that is very dominant in the family history. A dominant figure in this sense could be anyone that is the breadwinner, who is making important decisions or who serves as the main caregiver.

Infantile Embryonal Carcinoma

See Cancer, Gonad Problems, Yolk Sac Tumor

Infertility

See Alcoholism, Addictions (Drug), Chlamydia, Endometriosis, Estrogen Problems, Female Problems Fever, Gonad Problems (Testicles), Hormone Problems, Inflammation / Infection, Male Problems, Miscarriage, Ovary Problems, Pineal Gland Problems, Radiation, Testosterone Problems, Toxins, Uterus Problems

Emotions

You feel unsettled by deep emotions that are surfacing from the past. These emotions are related to ancestral trauma, making it more challenging for you to identify the origin of it. This is creating a great deal of emotional strain and inner conflict. You may feel like you are a victim within a situation that is out of your control. You have had your fair share of blame and responsibility for other's mishaps and shortcomings. You might feel intimidated by the idea of becoming a parent. Sometimes your partners' fears could also influence how you are feeling about becoming a parent. Your partner might have a fear of becoming a parent. Your own childhood may have been traumatizing, causing you to fear repeating the same mistakes as your parents. There is a deep fear of sabotaging your relationship with your future child.

Inflammation / Infection

See Arthritis, Bacteria, Bursitis, Mastoiditis, Rheumatoid Arthritis

Emotions

You are not letting go of a past or current conflict (or trauma) with someone or due to a confrontational circumstance. You are dwelling on issues instead of being proactive in resolving it. You seem to be quite angry and fed-up. You may feel that if you let go of the anger then nothing will be done to change or resolve the circumstances. This is a sabotaging cycle. This may also be unresolved anger toward a parent or influential person, which is surfacing due to a more recent but unrelated issue. You feel powerless to change your circumstances. You feel great anger as no one is taking responsibility for the part they played in your life. You often blame others, just as you often feel like a victim of circumstance. You may feel that you just have to accept circumstances as they come. Influential people often dictate the direction of circumstances, which directly affects your quality of life. The anger and rage comes in waves when influential people or circumstances trigger your feelings of disempowerment and helplessness.

Insomnia

See Anxiety, Apnea, Depression, Mercury Poisoning, Narcolepsy, Pineal Gland Problems, Seasonal Adjustment Disorder, Sleep Problems

Emotions

There seem to be many unresolved issues that you feel unsure of how to approach and deal with. You often don't know how to take control of your life. You seem to be dwelling on issues for long periods of time without being proactive about it. Unconsciously, you feel less guilty by dwelling on unresolved issues even though you know there is something you need to figure out. You may lack the proper "tools" and understanding towards someone or a situation. You don't trust your own ability to resolve issues. You are facing circumstances in your life that are challenging your beliefs and capacity to cope with the emotions that are surfacing. You do not understand why you feel the way you do and you struggle to find your value within this conflicting situation.

Intercourse Pain / Problems

See Female Problems, Impotence, Male Problems, Pain, Pituitary Gland Problems, Uterus Problems

Emotions

There is a great deal of shame and guilt associated with your sexuality. You have been exposed to sex that was traumatic or disgusting. You may have experienced a very controlling childhood, causing you to feel unable to express yourself either sexually or emotionally. Sexuality was suppressed in the household and it was disgusting and dirty to abuse sex. Example: having sex with someone that you are not married to, or not in a relationship with. You may have experienced inappropriate interactions with influential people that may have made you feel a great deal of shame and guilt in regards to your sexuality. You might also be in a partnership where you feel unsafe or disconnected from your partner.

Intermittent Bleeding

See Menstruation

Interstitial Cystitis

See Anxiety, Bacteria, Bladder, Bladder Cancer, Female Problems, Incontinence, Inflammation, Menopause, Male Problems, Muscle Problems

Emotions

You may feel intense anger and rage, holding on to a desire for vengeance. You refuse to let go of past anger. A family member has to pay and answer for the pain and struggle they have caused. You are very upset with an authority figure (either a parent or guardian) that challenged you and may have abused you in one way or another. You seem to have been aware from a young age that the behavior of this influential person was morally wrong or just plain unfair. You have immense resistance giving in to authority, as authority in your opinion is incompetent, stupid and just plain evil. You seem desperate to regain your own personal power. You feel that your personal power has been taken away. The anger is motivated by feeling powerless and out of control. You feel excluded from making important decisions that have a direct impact on you.

Intestinal Cramps

See Cramps, Colon Problems, Diarrhea, Inflammation, Intestine Problems, Muscle Problems, Nausea, Pain, Toxins

Emotions

You may be fearful of moving forward in your life. You have had negative experiences in the past whenever you tried to move forward. You feel conflicted, longing for a change of circumstance, yet resistant to changing stubborn patterns and routines. You do not feel that you fit into the bigger picture. You typically either sabotage or avoid situations that might cause you to feel vulnerable or exposed.

Interstitial Pneumonitis

See Acute Interstitial Pneumonitis, Asbestos, Lung Problems

Intestine (Small Intestine) Problems

See Candida, Celiac Disease, Colon Cancer, Colon Problems, Constipation, Cramps, Digestive Problems, Hernia, Irritable Bowel Syndrome, Stomach, Toxins

Emotions

You've experienced circumstances and people's reactions toward you in a very intense manner. You have many communication blocks with the family and feel misunderstood. You access your motivation and passion from a fighting instinct, which causes more tension than necessary. The instincts are activated by old trauma, causing you to make decisions that result in self-sabotaging patterns. You often find yourself in self-created stressful situations. You should make more judgment calls from the heart mind. You feel disconnected from yourself and not sure what to make of the circumstances. You went through a big change and transition in your life. You have become stuck as a result of fear and a lack of trust in yourself and loved ones.

Ileum

You feel as though you are only allowed to have and enjoy the left overs in life. You feel that you must allow others to do as they please while you are stuck and stagnant in a restrictive role.

Irritable Bowel Syndrome

See Anxiety, Colitis, Colon Cancer, Colon Problems, Digestive Problems, Hernia, Intestine Problems

Emotions

You have felt suppressed in everything you've tried to accomplish. Influential people did not give you the support and validation you needed in order to safely express yourself. You feel held back, as you do not know if you have permission to venture outside of the family's values and belief system. You may be holding on to all your negative experiences in life. This may be the result of a childhood where influential people never had enough time or patience to listen and acknowledge you. You are holding on to what you want to say just in case you have an opportunity to express it one day.

IBS with symptoms Diarrhea

This may indicate that you have an intense and stressful relationship with your mother or father. The pattern and stress you had with your parents is repeating itself in your current personal relationships. You often felt under attack, abused or rejected by authority figures when all you needed was to feel safe and secure.

IBS with symptoms Constipation

This may indicate that you have experienced abuse or very hostile actions from those you relied on for survival (especially during infancy stages). You are holding on to negative experiences as a result of abuse and hostility. You may have an unconscious fear of letting go of the trauma because it may cause old cycles to surface again.

Itching

See Anxiety, Allergies, Inflammation, Parasites, Rashes, Skin Problems, Toxins

Emotions

Your self-sabotaging patterns are causing you a great deal of frustration. You are aware of how fears and past blocks are holding you back. It's causing you immense irritation, as you are unsure of how to move forward, away from it. You fear that you might fail making changes and that your support system (people in your life) might fail you, as well. You are having a hard time believing in your talents.

Jaundice in new born / child

See Hepatitis, Liver Problems, Skin Problems

Emotions

While in utero, the baby may have sensed there were many challenges in store after birth. The child may have felt very resistant to being born and deal with circumstances that would be challenging. The birth trauma seemed to have triggered awkwardness, fear, anger and rebellion against influential forces. The baby seems to be quite stressed as a result of the new environment and may feel unprotected. They feel irritated and agitated by new influential people, threatened with a fear of being verbally attacked or in danger. There is an ancestry line where alcohol was abused which caused a great deal of trauma to the liver. The trauma of the birth (being squeezed through the birth canal) may have triggered liver problems in the newborn baby. The ancestor's suppressed emotions were stored in the liver. This may now have surfaced in the baby's liver. Trauma experienced during the birth triggered these old traumas from the ancestry line. It's a collective consciousness of anger, resentment, hostility and trauma of alcohol abuse, all triggered in in a new generation.

Jaw Grinding / Clenching

See Temporomandibular Joint and Muscle Disorder (TMJD) / Jaw Grinding / Clenching

Jaw Problems

See Temporomandibular Joint and Muscle Disorder (TMJD)

Jaw Cancer is often related to speaking the truth and finding the words twisted by authority figures. You felt ignored, as if what you had to say was invalid. This created a great deal of stress on the jaw line. There was no power in your words.

Jeunes Syndrome

See Bone Problems, Congenital Disorders, Muscle Problems, Poisoning, Toxins

Joint Problems

See Arthritis, Back Problems, Bursitis, Cumulative Trauma Disorder, Cyst, Heel Spurs, Inflammation, Myofascial Pain Syndrome (MPS), Osteoarthritis, Pelvic Problems, Shoulder Problems, Reactive Arthritis, Rotator Cuff Problems, Rheumatoid Arthritis, Tendon Problems

Emotions

You have a great deal of resentment and anger related to your perceived shortcomings in life. This could be issues related to personal relationships and failed projects; old past incidents are still an issue. There may be current situations that have triggered unresolved issues from the past. You may feel stagnant in these circumstances and rigid about changing or resolving these issues. This may cause you to feel trapped and angry. You feel forced to deal with things as they come, rather than getting your way. This makes you resentful because you cannot have what you want. The family may have created a great deal of drama and projected responsibilities onto you, leaving you no freedom of choice. This caused conflict for you because you felt pushed around and attacked (either verbally or physically) by loved ones.

Discussed in Volume 1: Crackling Joints, Shoulder joint, Hip joint, Wrist joint, Finger joint, Voluntarily cracking joints / fingers, Ankle joint, Toe joints

Kaposi Sarcoma

See HIV, Cancer, Herpes, Tumors, Virus

Emotions

You feel deeply ashamed of the unwanted attention your illness has brought upon you. You are disgusted with yourself and are acutely aware of people's reactions towards you. You feel overly sensitive as to how others see and perceive you. You resent being in this situation and feel persecuted by the world for being here. Your current environment and the relationships you have with others reinforce the feeling that you are a bad person. You have come to a point where you just want to be left alone and therefore, push others away. Your internalized anger has come to the surface and you feel like you should be punished.

Keloid

See Attacked, Skin Problems

Emotions

You seem to be carrying and physically revealing a great deal of persecution and punishment trauma from your ancestry. You feel intense emotions that have begun to transition from an emotional state to a physical state. Your built-up emotions are swelling to the surface. You feel an immense sense of injustice and feel wronged by society as a result of your gender within the culture. Your culture has been suppressed and abused for many generations. You are very sensitive to judgment and often overreact to criticism or being reprimanded. You have a deep unconscious need to overcompensate for times when influential people suppressed your boundaries and opinions.

Kennedy's Disease (also known as Spinal and Bulbar Muscular Atrophy)

See Duchenne Muscular Dystrophy, Female Problems, Huntington's disease, Infertility, Male Problems, Motor Neuron Disease, Muscle Dystrophy, Muscle Problems, Myofascial Pain Syndrome (MPS), Nerve problems, Pelvic Problems, Pituitary Problems, Spinal Cord, Testosterone Problems

Emotions

What you experience in your environment has a big impact on how you feel. Deep trauma related to feeling out of control is related to this condition. You need to be in control of everything; when you are not in control you feel as if you have no purpose and everything will fall apart. You feel that you have been relied on far too much by others. You have a caring nature and will do what you can for others. Your generosity and need to be in control can cause immense inner conflict. You may overload yourself with chores and responsibilities, often secretly resenting those people whom you are supporting. You want your needs to be attended to, as well. You feel a sense of guilt over past issues yet know that you can do nothing to change the outcome—what's done is done

Keratoconus

See Eye Problems

Kerion Celsi

See Fungus, Parasites, Rashes, Skin Problems, Tinea Capitis

Emotions

You are rejecting your own needs. The environment and personal relationships are causing you to feel very irritated, invaded or controlled. You feel sensitive towards influential people and the actions directed your way. The more problems there are in your surroundings, the more sensitive, irritated and stressed you feel. You often feel attacked by others for being yourself. You feel shameful and unacceptable because you have been made to feel guilty for you behavior in the past.

Kidney Problems

See Blood Pressure (High), Cancer, Hypertension, Mercury Poisoning, Kidney Cancer, Kidney Stones, Sickle Cell, Uremia

Emotions

The kidneys store a great deal of anger and resentment. You often feel very upset due to old abandonment and rejection trauma. You seem to always expect the worst. You may have found yourself in a situation or partnership that is triggering old abandonment and rejection trauma. The fear surfaces in the form of resentment and anger. Anger and resentment is your most powerful defense and keeps threatening situations and people at bay. You use resentment to fight against challenges. You often feel as though you've wasted time chasing unsuccessful relationships and goals.

Kidney Stones

See Kidney Problems

Emotions

You seem to feel a great amount of anger. The anger and resentment have been piling up, one on top of the other. New anger is added to old anger, resulting in rage and grief, as you do not know how to resolve this mountain of emotions. You haven't dealt well with circumstances that caused you to lose your personal space and territory. You feel angry and resentful for failing to express firm boundaries toward influential people. You are deeply saddened by not being able to fight off or resolve certain issues and relationships. You have taken the blame for everything that has gone wrong.

Klinefelter's Syndrome discussed in Volume 1.

See Infertility, Learning Disability, Male Problems, Nerve Problems, Speech, Stuttering, Testosterone Problems

Knee Problems

See Bone Problems, Inflammation, Joint Problems, Tendon Problems

Emotions

You have found yourself stuck in an uncomfortable situation. You don't have an actionable plan to move forward on a project or in your personal life. Your perception of the future is mixed up with your own inner fear and dread of being ridiculed, judge or rejected. You fear being judged by family members if you follow your dreams. You feel disempowered by life due to a past failure that left you feeling judged, humiliated and attacked (either verbally or physically) by others.

Köhler Disease discussed in Volume 1.

See Bone Problems, Cramps, Muscle Problems, Weight Problems

Labor Pain

See Anxiety, Birth, Muscle Problems, Pain, Pelvic Problems, Tendon Problems

Emotions

You may feel very rigid and afraid to give birth. This is not a pleasant experience and the thought of it is enough to scare anyone! The more rigid, tense or scared you are, the more tensed the muscles will be. You have a fear of losing control and often contract your muscles to protect and shield yourself from pain. You may be feeling guilt towards someone or a situation and seem to feel rigid about resolving it.

Lactic Acidosis

See Anemia, Anxiety, Hyperventilation, Hypoxia, Hypotension, Vomiting

Emotions

You are very controlled and under pressure by influential people. In the past, you were forced to accept responsibilities and complete unpleasant tasks that were not intellectually stimulating. You may still feel pressured and controlled even though circumstances may have changed. As a result, you don't find any joy or happiness in what you do. The pressure to be successful was projected by influential people. Expectations were communicated to you by means of dramatic threats or insults that made you feel stressed and confused.

Lactose Intolerance

See Allergies

Emotions

This condition may be related to a hostile, cold and emotionally absent bonding phase between you and your mother after birth. Your mother may have been traumatized, exhausted or not ready to become a mother. She may also have suffered from postnatal depression affecting the bonding stages. Your mother may have unconsciously resented you (ancestral trauma). Sensing this, you may have associated being fed milk with feeling of hostility, rejection and anger. These emotions may be activated every time you consume milk products, unconsciously taking them back to those first associations with milk.

Laryngitis

See Inflammation

Emotions

Influential people are suppressing your truth. You fear judgment and critiques from others if you express what you really need to say. What you want to say has become urgent, but no one is listening or paying attention. Your voice and truth have been (figuratively) suppressed for long enough. You may have associated expressing yourself with trauma, such as punishment by a controlling and dominating figure. You have attracted people that project the same controlling and dominating qualities as the influential people in your past. This has made you afraid to speak up although you are deeply angered for being silenced.

Larynx Cancer

See Cancer, Throat Problems

Emotions

There is no power in your words. Influential people stripped you of your confidence and ability to exercise freedom of speech. You were not able to express clear boundaries, nor were you able to exercise it during debates. Communication was always accompanied with conflict and verbal attacks. An influential person always sidestepped and invalidated you whenever you tried to express your feelings.

Lead Poisoning

See Poisoning, Toxins

Learning Problems

See ADHD, Autism, Dyslexia, Klinefelter's Syndrome, Tic

Emotions

You have made an association that life is dangerous, including learning information about the world and those in it. You have an unconscious fear that you will become contaminated while learning what about life and history. This association was made during very early developmental stages. You feel safe with what you have learned and experienced so far on your own. You may have experienced a trauma that caused one of your survival instincts to become activated. This instinct did not switch off, as the trauma was not completed. You are now stuck in a survival instinct, which causes you to focus on the past and how to survive future obstacles. You fear that new experiences will recreate the trauma. You may have experienced a trauma when you were concentrating and focusing on something. As a result, you feel unsafe to be still and focused.

Leg Problems

See Circulation Problems, Cramps, Muscle Problems, Paralyzed, Skeletal System, Tic

Emotions

You are angry and frustrated because you feel controlled whenever you try to express yourself. You fear moving away from old habits even though the habits themselves may be debilitating. You have learned how to transform debilitating habits into patterns that serve you. These are patterns you developed based on negative experiences. You have been pushed and held to high expectations since childhood. You have been pushed hard during childhood with high expectations. You are very set in your ways and fear that if you change your patterns, you may lose control of your routines. Your stubbornness often gives you a false sense of power. Your life is changing as the stubbornness turns into self-sabotaging patterns that cause you anger and frustration.

Leprosy

See Bacteria, Eye Problems, Nerve Problems, Skin Problems

Emotions

You have felt unwelcome in the world, with a sense of guilt just for existing. You regret not taking advantage of opportunities that have come your way. You now realize you should have because these missed opportunities may have changed things for the better. You are deeply saddened, with a long history of punishment, persecution, blame or abuse trauma. You have given into the pressure of influential people and become someone that does not resonate with you. Your true identity was not accepted or validated. You have allowed yourself to become disempowered and overwhelmed by forces that are more powerful. You live in the past, wondering how you could have changed things and altered certain outcomes.

Leukemia

See Acute Lymphoblastic Leukemia, Blood Problems, Cancer, Heart Problems

Emotions

You may feel attacked (either verbally or physically) from all angles and have no way of escaping. You do not know how to handle challenging obstacles, causing you to feel weak and unsupported without any guidance or structure. . You feel even more challenged by how your circumstances made you feel. You often get sucked into life's drama and are unable to find your footing. You feel around and do not feel safe. You often struggle to establish and find your personal space. You have fought a hard inner battle and now are worn-out and tired. Your defenses are weak and you feel you can't defend yourself against influential people. Where you should find safety instead there is nothing but hostility, blame and abuse. You find it confusing and stressful to communicate. Your foundation feels as if it's built on unstable and debilitating emotions. You often feel under attack; invaded by the harshness and selfishness of others.

Lipoma

See Tumor

Emotions

You feel the need to overly protect yourself from negative influential people. You may feel that no matter what you do, you cannot escape your circumstances. You feel stuck and your suppressed emotions are rising to the surface. This causes you to feel as if you are slowly starting to lose control over your life. You are overwhelmed with resentment and anger toward people who are abusing your goodwill. This is often a guardian, parent, family or long-term partner. You thought they had your best interests at heart until you realized too late that you were left unsupported and taken advantage of.

Lisping

See Sinus Problems, Speech Problems

Emotions

This condition may have been brought on by a medical condition, if so explore the possibility of the medical condition first. Lisping in this case would only be a secondary symptom and not the original problem. You may have experienced a traumatic incident that caused you to freeze in time. You want to go back to a time when you felt safe and protected, often back to the womb stages. You may feel you had a better relationship and connection with your parents while in the womb as you felt more buffered and protected.

Lips

Emotions

You have a fear of judgment if you say what you really want to say. You choose to say what others want to hear, as this is the safest way to communicate. You may have been wronged, attacked or judged for saying things that do not support another's opinion. You do not feel listened to. You are insecure about communicating your needs and feel challenged to express yourself.

Liver Cancer

See Alcoholism, Cancer, Cirrhosis, Hepatitis, Hypoxia, Liver Cancer, Mercury Poisoning, Poisoning, Toxins

Emotions

This condition is often related to ancestral trauma related to a lack of food, poverty or a lack of emotional needs being met. You may feel as though you were treated unfairly. Everyone else had it easy and was favored more than you were. You didn't get your share and feel like an outcast in your own family. Your conflict with the family makes you feel isolated and pushed away. You used aggression and rage to defend yourself, making yourself very unpopular. You feel conflicted because you want to express yourself, but the cost is too high. You regret things you've said and done in the past and want to make peace with your past.

Liver Problems

See Alcoholism, Cancer, Cirrhosis, Hepatitis, Hypoxia, Liver Cancer, Mercury Poisoning, Poisoning, Toxins

Emotions

Emotionally, you are very calm; however there can be cases where people go to the opposite extreme. You find it challenging to connect with your inner voice so you search for substances and people to fill the void within. You are bitter about the way your life has panned out. You were often confused by your mother's (or prominent female figure's) inconsistent behavior. You are still waiting for the love you didn't get as a child. Your mother may have had a challenging relationship with her partner and this had a direct influence on you. A great deal of your anger is as a result of unresolved issues between you and your parents.

Low Blood Pressure

See Blood Pressure Low

Lung Cancer

See Asbestos, Cancer, Lung Problems, Pain, Polyps, Toxins

Emotions

If the cancer has already spread to the bones begin by addressing issues related to the lungs and then move onto the Bone Problems section. You feel beaten and run down by the past and your inner strength is weak from holding back grief, unhappiness and feeling choked by life. You feel that your need for love is not met by anyone, no matter how hard you work for it. You have had to stand strong mostly on your own during hardships, with only yourself to rely on and confide in. You are grieving for the lack of understanding, compassion and intimacy of partners that you've have had in life. Your fear of being loved often sabotaged personal relationships.

Lung Problems

See Acute Interstitial Pneumonitis, Asthma, Bronchitis, Hypertension, Hyperventilation, Hypoxia, Lung Cancer, Pneumonia, Tuberculosis (TB)

Emotions:

If the lungs had a voice, it would often be very cheery and happy. If they are quiet and seem like they are hiding then it's because their owner is storing a lot of grief, old sorrow, anxiety or depression, even suppressed fears. The lungs have a need to express emotions when they are detected. If sadness and grief is stored for long periods of time then it can physically cause a great deal of physical discomfort.

The lungs are signaling to you that you need to deal with your stuff!

Collapsed lung

The suppressed grief and lack of joy in life has taken its toll. This is often combined with ancestral grief. You feel that your inner strength failed in the past. You suffered trauma related to feeling unwelcome in life, especially after birth. It is as if you are a triangle trying to fit into a square hole.

Lupus

See Anemia, Attack, Auto Immune Disease, Blood Problems, Kidney Problems, Muscle Problems, Skin Problems, Tendon Problems

Emotions

There may have been an abusive incident within the family, whether it was directed at you or not, it may have affected you to a great extent. You feel under attack (either verbally or physically) by your own blood (family members and people that are close to you). Influential people dominated you to such an extent that you have given your power away. Fighting against authority figures is useless. Long-term abuse or punishment may have caused you to believe that you deserve to be punished, humiliated, abandoned or rejected. You feel powerless to change the cycle of circumstances in your life.

Lyme's Disease

See Asthma, Bacteria, Fatigue, Heart Problems, Inflammation, Joint Problems, Nerve Problems, Parasites, Rheumatoid Arthritis

Emotions

You have given a great deal of time and energy to loved ones and various projects. Immense gratification follows when you work hard. It allows you to feel connected to your purpose and identity, which makes you feel safe, valued and important. As a result, you feel overly responsible at work, home and towards meeting people's needs. Your hard working nature tries to accommodate everyone and everything.

Lymphoma

See Cancer, Immune System Compromised,

Emotions

You often feel overlooked and devalued by influential people. You have a deep need to feel safe when you are loved. You have made a negative association with receiving attention, as love may not have been shown to you in a healthy way. You are afraid you've failed the expectations of influential people and you cannot forgive yourself for that. In your mind, failure = abandonment, isolation or being treated as an outcast. Love is toxic, yet you cannot move away from circumstances or relationships that are toxic. You want love, however you often attract people and situations that make you feel devalued. What is your definition of love? Do people in your life make you feel the way you described love? Which area of the body is affected and refer to the Quick Reference Guide for more information.

Lymphatic Filariasis

See Adenoids, Immune System Compromised, Inflammation / Infection, Lymphatic System, Parasites

Emotions

You feel a great need to insulate yourself from your environment. You feel unsafe and targeted for a possible verbal attack as a result of moody influential people. Other people's action and words leave you feeling invaded yet you feel helpless to change the situation as no one listens to or respects your boundaries. You may have been left to fend for yourself. Your parents may have been emotionally or physically absent, creating in you a constant fear of abandonment. You have suppressed your ability to express boundaries. In your mind, expressing boundaries might result in people rejecting or punishing you by withholding the love and attention you need. As a result, you feel invaded by people's needs and demands, as your own needs are not being met.

Lymphatic System Compromised

See Immune System Compromised, Poisoning, Toxins

Emotions

You often feel stuck in a circumstance or under attack without the ability to speak up for yourself. You don't feel worthy of speaking up. Speaking up may result in condemnation, isolation or cause you to be ignored and isolated. You have a very deep need to be accepted for who you are, however this need has not been met in a healthy way by influential people. You are tired and drained from trying to be accepted. You are vulnerable and have lost a great deal of self-confidence. You are processing shame as a result of being unable to meet any goals or achieve the success you want. Your self-sabotaging patterns have become debilitating, often causing you psychological harm. You can't let go of past hurts and keep wondering how you could have dealt with things differently. You are going through the "what if" phase and need to let go, as this is causing you more emotional stress.

Malaria

See Fever, Inflammation, Liver Problems, Nausea, Parasites

Emotions

Malaria is caused by a parasite, it begs the question, "Who are the parasites in your life? Who or which circumstances are draining you?" People often attract parasites in human form (as well as taxing circumstances) that may take advantage. You have an already weak immune system, which makes you more susceptible to being affected by parasites. This is also a reflection of poor or unclear boundaries towards people in your environment. You allowed yourself to be attacked either verbally or physically. You may have a fear of setting boundaries, as you might be rejected, abandoned or punished if you do. You seem to feel unsafe and unsure of your position within the family. Something or someone might have threatened the flow of love you received from a parent or loved one. You may have felt like you had to keep it all together in your personal life. You don't feel that others respect choices you've made. You often have to play along with someone else's rules, suppressing your goals and freedom. This may have caused you to feel trapped, overprotected or controlled. Your need for freedom was met by feeling controlled, suffocated or trapped.

Male Problems

See Gonads, Hormone Problems, Mid Life Crisis, Penis Problems, Peyronie's Disease, Prostate Problems, Testosterone Problems

Emotions

You are very critical and self-conscious of your identity and masculinity. You seem to find your role as a male figure quite challenging. There are many expectations, rules and standards that you have to follow in order to be accepted by your parents, females and society. You often feel guilt and shame whenever you explore any of your feminine qualities because this is seen as a weakness. You may fear the feminine qualities will cause you to come across as weak and vulnerable to attack. Men were always seen as the provider, leader, authority and dominant figure. With these titles come a great deal of responsibility, burdens and a need to provide. You feel that the success of the family's health, education and nurturance weighs heavily on your shoulders. There is a great deal of shame and humiliation related to not being able to live up to the expectations of influential people. This may be a result of losing a job, income or prominent position.

Malnutrition

See Anorexia, Anxiety, Bulimia, Depression, Digestive Problems, Marasmus, Tremor

Emotions

You are rebelling against everything that you cannot control in life. Your ability to control your environment has not given you any satisfaction. Losing control and the emotions associated with that has caused you to turn inward. You seem to be lost in life, without a purpose, almost as if you don't want to be here anymore. Trauma related to rejection has greatly challenged your self-esteem and the ability to feel strong as a separate and independent person. Now you are rejecting yourself. You have shown very little interest in life and in the activities that you once loved. You feel unworthy of happiness and are depriving yourself of the good things in life as a form of punishment. You have become increasingly stubborn and do not want to play by the rules anymore. You are trying to take a stand against someone whom you have held a grudge against for some time now.

Mania

See Anxiety, Bi-Polar, Depression, Hyperthyroidism, Hysteria

Emotions

Mania is often the end result of long-term emotional suppression (often related to ancestral trauma). There is a great deal of turmoil in the family and ancestry line that has never been expressed. The parent of the child that is affected by mania has been confronted with this challenging situation in order to explore what they have not expressed in their life and childhood. This condition is more related to ancestral trauma however; the parents of the client (if client is a child) should explore their own past. The child is reflecting certain characteristics of the parents that need to be explored in the parent.

Marasmus discussed in Volume 1.

See Anorexia, Anxiety, Bulimia, Depression, Digestive Problems

Mastoiditis

See Bacteria, Hearing Impairment, Inflammation, Middle Ear Infection

Emotions

You might feel caught between rivalries that have grown out of control between parents or other authority figures in your life. You do not want to hear what is going on around you and are scared and uncertain of your position in the family. You can feel and sense the hostility in the environment but feel stuck with no way out. Your parents often play you off of the other parent by saying demeaning things.

Maxillary Sinus discussed in Volume 1.

See Eye Problems, Inflammation, Pressure in Body, Sinus Problems

Melanoma

See Blood Problems, Cancer, Lymph Nodes, Skin Cancer, Toxins

Emotions

You are often reluctant to express emotions. You draw strength from the ability to suppress, be strong and endure challenges. You have a great fear of exposing any weaknesses. You sweep emotions under the carpet and are a "people pleaser." You feel overwhelmed by people's demands and allow others to get under your skin. You may come across as very calm, yet you feel a great deal of resentment and anger which is eating away at you.

Melasma

See Estrogen, Menopause, Ovarian Cancer, Pregnancy, Thyroid Problems

Emotions

Change is dangerous. You have had negative experiences when you entered a new phase in life, which forced you to change yourself or your environment. Your ancestors may also have come under scrutiny, abuse or punishment when they had to move from their homes or colonies to a new environment by force or threats. Your environment is challenging your ability to feel and be in control, as it all seems to be changing now. These changes could include giving birth to a child, being forced to make career changes, ending relationships or enduring very stressful times that challenge self-worth. It is often related to trauma of losing control of one's environment and safe place.

Meniere's Disease

See Abasia, Hearing Impairment, Vertigo, Tinnitus

Emotions

You may be feeling all over the place, emotionally, physically and spiritually. You often feel threatened by your circumstances and future events that have not taken place. You seem to have trouble identifying the implications of recent decisions that were made. You feel confused in regard to the next step in life and are tired of carrying other people's baggage. You have had enough of carrying the responsibilities of others. If you let go of the responsibilities, you fear you will lose your value within the family. Your identity is associated with being responsible. You may also fear losing the love and admiration of those that rely on your hard work.

Meningitis

See Bacteria, Back, Coxsackie Virus, Reye's Syndrome

Emotions

You may not feel accepted for who you are and what you have become. You feel regularly rejected by everyone that you interact with due to patterns of rejection within the family. You often feel you are to blame for everything. You do not feel like you have a leg to stand on when someone blames you for a mistake that was not your fault. You want to restore the right to be treated with respect, however you feel unworthy enough to do so. You are aware that your living arrangements are unhealthy, yet you do not speak up about it. Your childhood programming made you believe that you have to accept what an adult or senior person says and that is final.

Menopause

See Estrogen, Female Problems, Hormone Problems, Melasma, Mid Life Crisis

Emotions

You seem to have a fear of aging, being undesirable or not being needed anymore. You often feel resentful toward men as you don't feel desired any more. You believe that after you have reached menopause there is no turning back, "I am getting old now, my days of fun are over." Your value and purpose in life feels challenged by this condition. Many women express their value through their fertility and once that has stopped, they feel they have no purpose. Even though you may not have had children, knowing that you have the power to bear a child is empowering. It could feel like an ending of your purpose and value in life. You may be resenting your body and feeling betrayed by it.

Menstrual Problems

See Anxiety, Anorexia, Cyst, Fatigue, Fibroids, Hormone Problems, Hyperthyroidism, Infertility, Malnutrition, Ovarian Cyst, Pituitary Gland Problems, Polyps, Pregnancy, Thyroid Problems, Weight Problems

Emotions

You cannot accept who you are along with your feminine qualities. You may see it as a disadvantage. You seem to resent the process that women have to go through. You may also be engaged in a battle of the wills with your mother. There seems to be power games being played back and forth. You may resent your mother due to a confused or dysfunctional upbringing and feel that your parents should have known better. You may have felt like you had to be the parent during childhood. You also seem to be caught up in a love-hate relationship with influential female figures. Your mother's partner may have abused her and as a result, she took her frustrations out on you.

Mercury Poisoning

See Fever, Hair Loss, Insomnia, Nausea, Skin Problems Sweating, Kidney Problems, Poisoning, Teeth Problems, Toxins, Tremor

Emotions

You feel challenged by the intensity of your anger. The more anger you are holding on to, the more severe the mercury poisoning symptoms are. The more you let go of resentment, bitterness or anger, the easier it will be for the body to release mercury. Mercury stored in the brain tissue causes a foggy head and bad memory. It begs the question, "What are you trying to forget or not focus on in your life?"

Migraine

See Atlas Problems, Head Ache, Hearing Impairment, Nausea, Sinus Problems, Tinnitus
Emotions
People who suffer from intense migraines often have poor personal boundaries. You don't know when to say "yes" and when to say "no." You often end up saying "yes" when actually you want to say "no." You end-up in conflicting circumstances that you cannot escape from. You always feel, "Should I stay or should I go?" You sabotage your ability to express clear boundaries. This makes you feel resentful toward yourself, your circumstances and the people who are taking advantage of you.

Middle Ear Infection

See Hearing Impairment, Inflammation / Infection, Mastoiditis
Emotions
You seem to feel stuck and held back by influential people. This does not seem to have had a positive outcome for you. You do not trust your own judgment, as it seems to be failing. You seem to be reverting back to a time where you learned certain values or survival strategies and you are now holding on to it. This is not serving you in a positive way. You have become stuck with old and stagnant ideas and concepts. Your rigidity and blocks are causing you a great deal of anger.

Mid Life Crisis

See Estrogen, Hormone Problems, Menopause, Testosterone Problems
Emotions
This is a phase that is sometimes inevitable to avoid. There are some who do get stuck feeling, "I don't have a purpose anymore or I don't fit in with society anymore." The first thing to acknowledge is that it is OK to go through this phase. Many people have successfully dealt with this phase. It is called the "Mid Life Crisis Phase," and it is exactly that—a phase. For some however, it feels like an end to a life cycle. It can feel like an important role as the adviser / guardian / breadwinner has stopped.

Miscarriage

See Pregnancy, Infertility, Hyperthyroidism, Abortion, Estrogen Problems, Eclampsia, Fallopian Tube Problems, Hysterectomy, Mercury Poisoning, Ovary Problems, Uterus Problems, Toxins
Emotions
This is an emotional experience and these circumstances can create immense tension and challenges within partnerships. This subject does not just concern the mother, as it involves the father as well. This situation might not be so traumatic to some (when the pregnancy was an accident or due to rape) and a heartache for others. The onset of this condition might indicate that there are unresolved issues between the mother and father that need to be

resolved, before bigger decisions such as having a child can be made.

Morning Sickness

See Nausea, Pregnancy

Emotions

Sometimes the new change that is about to take place can be an emotional and mental burden for most new mothers. This includes a mother that already has children. You may not be able to stomach the new changes and stress that is yet to come. People who release their stress levels in a healthy manner seem to have less of this side effect. In most cases, both you and your partner want the child. There may be some cases where there is only one person who really wants the child. This imbalance can create a lot of stress in the relationship and especially for the mother.

Motion Sickness

See Nausea, Morning Sickness

Emotions

You are sensitive and have stomached your fair share of ups and downs in life. You tend to be very emotional and as a result, often come across as dramatic (whether you intend to, or not). You feel like a victim when you have to deal with circumstances that are not favorable to you. You often feel pulled in two directions, trying to please everyone. You feel uneasy with and resistant to those in your environment who don't resonate with you. The motion sickness is a physical symptom of the body in an effort to escape and avoid any circumstance or environment that makes you feel uneasy, unsafe or threatened. You may feel conflicted with two different sources of information, which have been delivered. This could be a result of having your parents sharing their own individual opinion with you, leaving you confused about which opinion or instruction to heed and obey.

Motor Neuron Disease

See Attacked, Depression, Kennedy's Disease, Muscle Problems, Spine Problems

Emotions

MNDs are a group of neurological disorders that affect motor neurons. The most common MND is ALS or Lou Gehrig's disease. As it affects the nervous system, it will relate to communication issues and lack of control. The muscular system aspect relates to guilt and rigidity. There is a big part of you that has given up on achieving your goals. You may have had a project (or career) that took too much out of you – the emotional price you had to pay was too great. You do not feel noticed by influential people. During childhood, you felt that your parents never noticed you or paid you enough attention. You often felt that you were wasting away in front of everyone and no one even noticed. You may take on many responsibilities in the hopes of being acknowledged, loved and admired for carrying so many burdens. You want to show and prove to others that you are worth the energy and time invested in you. This could be a friendship, work commitment or partnerships.

Multiple Personality Disorder (MPD)

See Addictions, Alcoholism, Alzheimer's, Dementia, Depression, Huntington's Disease, Sexual Abuse

Emotions

You experienced a trauma that made part of your personality stuck in time. This personality or characteristic supported you, enabling you to survive trauma (this is often physical, sexual or severe mental abuse). You seem to revert back to a personality that served you whenever you were stressed and in need of comfort. You have associated this state of mind as a refuge during childhood. This personality (or personalities) provided support and safety. Your body mind and gut instinct memorized and associated this action and personality as a survival mechanism. Different traumas may have occurred, resulting in different personalities. Circumstances, smells, sounds, objects or people may trigger old traumas, making the personalities surface.

Multiple Sclerosis

See Attacked, Depression, Muscle Problems, Nerve Problems, Paralysis, Pelvic Problems, Spinal Cord, Tremor

Emotions

MS is caused by an auto-immune attack on the nervous system, causing demyelination or loss of myelin, the protective sheath around the nerves. Imagine a copper wire losing its plastic sheath. The same issue, which is a loss of signal (both communication and control) arises inside the body. You may have experienced trauma that made you feel helpless and unprotected. You overcompensate for feeling helplessness and unprotected during childhood by using anger to protect and defend yourself. There are cases when a client feels too scared and powerless to even express anger so they choose to become submissive.

Mumps

See Fever, Gonad Problems, Headache, Hearing Impairment, Infertility, Inflammation / Infection, Rash, Salivary Gland Disorders, Skin Problems, Virus

Emotions

You seem to be entering a stage where you are learning new information or adjusting to a new lifestyle. A new attitude toward life feels challenged by your relationship with influential people. Influential people may have challenged your self-worth by letting you understand your behavior is or was causing problems. You feel unsure of how to behave or have your needs met in a way that makes you feel safe. You may have been ashamed or manipulated into behaving a certain way, which left you feeling controlled, trapped or angry.

Muscle Problems

See Back Problems, Calcification, Cramps, Fibromyalgia, Hyperthyroidism, Myofascial Pain Syndrome (MPS), Pain, Pelvic Problems, Poisoning, Pressure in Body, Rotator Cuff Problems, Rupture, Shoulder Problems, Tendon Problems, Toxins

Emotions

Muscle weakness often represents an inner weakness due to a combination of emotional exhaustion, being overwhelmed or feeling rigid and guilty. You not only don't acknowledge your power; you seem to have abandoned it. You may be longing for a time when you had no problems and were free of stressful and angry people in your life. You seem to feel guilty about being the cause of problems within the family and feel blamed for many mistakes.

Muscular Dystrophy

See Duchenne Muscular Dystrophy, Kennedy's Disease, Motor Neuron Disease, Muscle Problems

Myalgic Encephalomyelitis (M.E)

See Apnea, Auto Immune, Chronic Fatigue, Sleep Disorders

Emotions

You do not feel listened to and may have a history of not being believed by others. You are trying hard to be acknowledged by loved ones and exhaust yourself with the amount of effort you invest in getting noticed. You crave the affection and recognition that you see others receive. You feel as if you have to climb mountains to be acknowledged because you do not feel worthy of receiving love and affection. You had a strict upbringing, with very little room for error. You feel very confused as to what others expect of you and often doubt your ability to meet the expectations of influential people. Nonetheless, you give it your best and often end up failing. This results as a manifestation of your worst fears.

Myasthenia Gravis

See Auto Immune, Eye Problems, Muscle Problems

Emotions

Your empowerment and will to live have been compromised and suppressed by your circumstances and trauma. You seem to feel stressed to the max and are in desperate need of rest. You may feel very resistant to continue your lifestyle with the way things are currently unfolding. Your body has taken a punch (figuratively). It does not want to be placed under more stress, strain and tension. This is often the result of a physiological issue, such as stressful working routines, abusive partnerships or childhood abuse. You may be sabotaging your progress. You were held back or punished in the past for starting projects and undertaking goals without the permission of influential people.

Myofascial Pain Syndrome (MPS)

See Back problems, Cramps, Cumulative Trauma Disorder, Dupuytren's Contracture, Hip Problems, Joint Problems, Muscle Problems, Neck Problems, Pelvic Problems, Shoulder Problems, Spine Problems

Emotions

You seem to feel overly sensitive to stress, pressure or feeling controlled and trapped as a result of your environment. You may have experienced a childhood where you never felt safe making decisions and have always felt alert and on guard. Your muscles were always tensed as you may have been stuck in a flight or fight mode. Relaxing is not safe and you have made an association that by being tensed you will survive challenges. It allows you to be on guard and protect yourself. You may have experienced times where influential people's moods were unpredictable. You were always on edge, with little time for yourself.

Myoma

See Estrogen, Female Problems, Fibroids, Menopause, Muscle Problems, Tumors, Uterus Problems, Weight Problems

Emotions

You seem to feel deeply resentful of what is happening to your body. The consequences have not caught up with the head mind. You are very angry that you cannot continue the life that you once knew. You seem to feel that your personality has changed, as well as the people around you. You do not want to go with the flow, with the direction the body is going in. You seem to resist the way that nature intended. You want to push back against your body clock.

Nail Biting

See Anxiety, Depression, Obsessive Compulsive Disorder (OCD)

Emotions

You seem to feel very insecure in your environment and relationships. You have a fear of expressing your anger because in your experience, aggressive people were often attacked and abandoned. You have been part of a stressful family that never quite got everything under control in life. You have seen influential people go off the wall when they felt overwhelmed, out of control or angry. This made you feel scared unprotected and very confused. Biting nails gives you an emotional relief from the stress that is taking place around you. Biting the nails is a distraction from your environment and an indirect outlet of anger that you are too afraid to voice. When you feel unsafe, threatened, or angry and out of control, you bite your nails.

Nail–Patella Syndrome discussed in Volume 1.

See Bone Problems, Hip Problems, Joint Problems, Kidney Problems, Knee Problems

Narcolepsy

See Apnea, Fatigue, Insomnia, Muscle Problems, Sleep Disorder

Emotions

You feel a desperate need to escape certain circumstances in your life as you've had enough and want to bail out. You often revert to a sleep state as you associate sleep with safety, peace and feeling protected. It's your way of dissociating from any trauma in your life. This could also be related to ancestral trauma. You may not have been allowed to say "no" during childhood and had to take things as they came. You are stuck in an old cycle. You often feel like a victim of circumstance and feel there is nothing that you can do about it. Sleep is the only saving grace.

Nausea

See Bacteria, Digestive Problems, Malaria, Mercury Poisoning, Migraine, Morning Sickness, Parasites, Ulcer, Virus

Emotions

What in your life are you unable to digest? Who and what are overwhelming you? You may feel challenged by past issues that are now being triggered by recent circumstances. You want to rid yourself of any toxic circumstances, including old emotions. Your head mind often creates a worst-case scenario that is not always real. The body is always ready to fight or flight and as a result, it produces too much gastric acid. This is also related to the vomiting instinct. The body tries to rid itself of excess acid. This can happen when a person tries to rid themselves of circumstances that are triggering old trauma. It's the body's way of trying to create a barrier between you and a stressful environment.

Vomiting

You need to get rid of toxic people, circumstances and relationships. There are no more benefits for you in these current circumstances and you might want to consider changing debilitating habits and patterns. You know what you need to do and where you need to go, yet you are fearful of the unknown and future. You triggered an instinct that requires you to move away from certain people, habits and circumstances to improve your quality of life. The body wants to rid itself of old toxic emotions and patterns.

Navel Problems

See Hernia – Umbilical Hernia, Intestines, Skin Problems

Emotions

You may feel invaded and irritated by your environment and loved ones. You crave nurturing, privacy and to be left in peace however your needs are being met by hostility, unpleasantness or invasive reactions of influential people. Feeling invaded can be personal space that is disrespected; it does not have to be physical. Your present circumstances are triggering a challenged relationship between mother and child. Your mother was not able to connect with you at birth perhaps due to exhaustion or maybe you were taken away immediately after birth.

Neck Problems

See Accidents, Back Pain, Cumulative Trauma Disorder, Upper Back, Middle Back, Lower Back, Muscle Problems, Myofascial Pain Syndrome (MPS), Pain, Shoulder Problems, Spine Problems, Whiplash

Emotions

You seem to feel rigid and need to control the outcome of everything you do. You feel that if you do not have the ability to control the environment, everything will go wrong. This will only make you feel obligated to fix everything again. This stems from a childhood where there was a great deal of pressure on you to understand concepts and situations that should not have been introduced until a later stage in your life. You may have observed your parents losing control of their own life and circumstances. You felt helpless and disempowered by the surrounding drama and conflict. When you feel out of control, you become rigid and afraid of failure or that a worst-case scenario might take place.

Necrosis

See Bites, Hypoxia, Inflammation / Infection, Pain, Poisons, Toxins

Emotions

The body feels poisoned, under attack and unable to defend itself. Is this how you feel emotionally, too? You may have been exposed to a harsh family environment that made you feel unsafe and unprotected by the world and influential people. Your negative environment had a big impact on your mental state, causing you to stew on negative thoughts, feelings of vengeance and resentment because of past injustices.

Necrotizing Fasciitis (flesh eating disease)

See Bacteria, Skin Problems, Virus

Emotions

This condition often starts when the immune system has been severely compromised. This could be the result of alcoholism, long-term illness or a condition that greatly challenged the immune system. You may have experienced a physical trauma that left an open wound that may have been the starting point of this condition. You seem to be feeling under attack and invaded by your environment. You may feel that it's dangerous to express boundaries and it is safer to allow others to just have their way. This way, you stay out of the firing line.

Nerve Problems

See Acoustic Neuroma, Arthritis, Bells Palsy, Carpal Tunnel Syndrome, Kennedy's Disease, Pain, Peripheral Nerve, Sciatica Nerve, Trigeminal Neuralgia

Emotions

You seem to feel unbalanced in your personal relationships and circumstances. You have difficulty expressing yourself and feel very misunderstood. You may find it challenging to listen to your gut instincts as well as establish your emotional needs. You have a hard time communicating with others, expressing your feelings. Instead, you often have silent angry fits or rage. This pattern may have developed from a childhood of having your words and actions closely monitored. You may have always been subject to scrutiny and felt like you couldn't ever do anything right. If this was not part of your childhood, it might be evident in your parents' immediate family. You have experienced trauma to the point that you have disconnected yourself from everything and everyone. This may also go to the other extreme. You may feel that you are not acknowledged or heard in a way that is satisfactory. This causes you to communicate too much, creating conflict and confrontation between yourself and rigid, influential people. This could also include physical activity. You find an outlet for your frustration by becoming active (such as participating in sports or games, for example) with the intention of releasing built-up tension and frustration.

Nervous Breakdown

See Adjustment Disorder, Anxiety, Depression, Hysteria, Obsessive Compulsive Disorder, Post-Traumatic Stress Disorder (PTSD), Seasonal Adjustment Disorder

Emotions

You may be feeling completely out of control. You have been experiencing long-term stress and have reached a point of exhaustion. Your body is burned out and tired. You may have been placed under a great deal of pressure during childhood to perform tasks where failure was not an option. If you failed, the stakes were high with abandonment, harsh criticism and hostility sure to follow as punishment. You are placing yourself under a great deal of pressure and take your role in life too seriously. You have temporarily lost touch with reality as a result.

Neuralgia

See Nerve Problems, Pain

Emotions

You seem to feel very lonely and angry as a result of influential people not taking the time to understand your needs. You feel ignored and rejected by the people you love. You may feel that you have been pushed aside, as you may have been a stubborn child. Your parents may have felt challenged by the your needs and felt unsure of how to interact with you. There was no tolerance for uniqueness and everything had to be systematic. This way of life did not resonate with you, making you feel isolated from the family. You do not have a choice other than to compromise with the way that things are going. You seem to be experiencing emotions on a very analytical level, instead of feeling with the heart mind.

Neurofibroma

See Nerve Problems, Pain, Tumors

Emotions

What you have learned and observed in your environment has caused a great deal of stress. You feel challenged by how the world and your family functions, which affects your motivation in life. You feel the need to run away and escape everything. You are unable to emotionally process your circumstances. The less you know about what is going on around you, the less stressed and tensed you are. Your rigidity and fear related to communicating yourself does not serve you well. As a result, you keep your own counsel.

Night Blindness

See Eye Problems

Nose Bleed

See Anxiety, Bleeding, Blood Problems, Nervous Breakdown

Emotions

Your character feels under attack by means of judgment, criticism or abuse. Your way of handling tasks and communicating are not accepted or approved by influential people. You feel temporarily disconnected from the joy in life, as you seem to focus too much on what others think of you. Your focus has been shifted away from the family or your partner. You are a people pleaser and focus too much on supporting others as you feel accepted and validated by pleasing people. The more you do for another, the more you feel valued and important. It also takes you further away from your accomplishments, as you are always busy pleasing others.

Nose - Bone

See Accidents, Bone Problems, Nose Bleed

Emotions

Structure of your nose often relates to your mother's relationships with her partner during your womb stages. Your mother may have felt rejected, pushed away or needed the protection of an emotionally unavailable partner. There seems to be a great need for the approval of a masculine figure. Resolve unresolved issues with a father figure.

Numbness

See Alcoholism, Back Problems, Carpal Tunnel Syndrome, Cumulative Trauma Disorder, Multiple Sclerosis, Neck Problems, Osteoporosis, Spine Problems, Tumor

Emotions

You do not want to continue a certain action, behavior, direction, role, relationship or activity. Your current circumstances bring you no joy. Instead, you feel resentful, as though you have no time for yourself and you feel controlled. You had to behave a certain way that would ensure safety and emotional survival (ancestral trauma). Your ability to be in the flow of life has been restricted by influential people and circumstances. You may have experienced trauma during childhood. This caused you to feel trapped and activated your frozen and paralyzed survival instinct. You have reverted to a state of numbness (freezing instinct) as it kept you safe to disconnect and dissociate from your environment and emotions. Feeling emotionally numb may have started to physically develop.

Obesity

See Weight Problems

Obsessive Compulsive Disorder (OCD)

See Anxiety, Cumulative Trauma Disorder, Nail Biting

Emotions

Repetitive behaviors may have given you mental and emotional relief from the stress that was taking place around you and within. Repeating certain behaviors are a distraction from your circumstances and how you feel. When you feel unsafe, threatened or out of control, you revert to an action or habit that made you feel safe in the past. This behavior or pattern has become a source of comfort whenever you are stressed or feel out of control. You found a survival pattern within a moment of trauma. You fear letting go of the habit or pattern because it is a reminder that you can cope and survive in stressful circumstances.

Onychophagia

See Anxiety, Nail Biting, Obsessive Compulsive Disorder (OCD)

Osteitis Pubis

See Cumulative Trauma Disorder, Inflammation, Hip Problems, Joint Problems, Muscle Problems, Pelvic Problems, Spine Problems

Note: Explore feeling under a great deal of pressure, control and in some cases, forced to achieve. You felt the need to be successful or pushed to be better than others. You feel pushed down and controlled by authority. Support was given and expressed in a way that may have been abusive. You feel a great deal of conflict with people that you consider yourself responsible for. Explore ancestral trauma related to the above mentioned as well.

Osteoarthritis

See Arthritis, Cumulative Trauma Disorder, Inflammation, Joint Problems, Pain, Reactive Arthritis, Rheumatoid Arthritis, Tendon Problems

Emotions

You have been so caught up in doing things for others that you often forgot to attend to your own needs. You have done so much for others that you have depleted your energy and resources; you are running on empty. This makes you resentful of others for taking your time and also angry with yourself for not taking time to enjoy life. You may have experienced a childhood where you felt forced or obligated to do things that did not resonate with you. This may have caused you to do activities while feeling angry, resentful or rigid. Therefore, these activities brought you no joy.

Osteomalacia

See Alcoholism, Bone Problems, Osteoporosis, Skeletal System

Emotions

You feel a need to hide, as you often feel exposed and unprotected. Your environment has been challenging and a mother's love has not been very nurturing. Your support system is unreliable, making you feel unable to accomplish any of your goals. You may feel snowed under by life's responsibilities, rules, regulations and the needs of others. You feel that everyone wants something from you and you are running out of resources to hide how you truly feel. Your need for support was met by lack and not having enough of anything that you want or need. You may worry that everything could cave in at any minute.

Osteoporosis

See Alcoholism, Bone Cancer, Bone Problems, Osteo-Malacia

Emotions

You are trying to avoid being controlled by people at all cost. You feel resistant to compromise as in the past, compromise has often left you holding the short end of the rope, which leaves you angry and resentful. You have reached a point where you may be desperate to feel free from all the negative thoughts and emotions. Your emotions are getting the best of you. You have become stubborn as a way of protecting yourself from the high expectations of those around you and setting a boundary. You feel challenged by the idea of forgiving people that have challenged you and caused you harm.

Ovarian Cyst

See Cyst, Cancer, Ovary Cancer / Problems, Polycystic Ovary Syndrome

Emotions

Emotions such as resentment have grown out of control. You may be consumed by the unjust treatment and behavior of others (relationship with your mother or a partner). You don't feel that you are permitted to put a stop to people's behavior, which is upsetting to you. You may have been made to believe that women have to obey, listen and always compromise for the sake of other's needs—emotional, physical or intimate. You are rebelling against projections and expectations from influential people and fighting off dominant figures. You seem to feel that your mother or an influential female is a sore reminder of how disempowered women are. Abusive and domineering people are a part of your life.

Ovary Problems / Cancer

See Birth, Bleeding, Cyst, Estrogen Problems, Fallopian Tube Problems, Female Problems, Hysterectomy, Hot Flushes, Melasma, Menstrual Problems, Menopause, Uterus

Emotions

You have been suppressing sexual anger. You do not feel worthy of having your own sexual needs met and you often feel obligated to put the needs of others ahead of your own. You may feel invaded by men whose needs are selfish, making you feel unable to receive the love and intimacy you desire. You may be grieving for missed opportunities to be a mother or feel that you failed in your role as a mother. Being a mother didn't work out the way that you intended. You may not feel good enough in the eyes of influential male figures. You may have been shamed and made to feel less valued than other people in your life. You have been belittled and demeaned by influential people over a long period of time making you uncertain as to where you fit in the family and society, in general.

Oxygen Problems (Lack of)

See Hypoxia, Birth – Oxygen Deprivation

Paget's Disease

See Arthritis, Bone Problems, Hip Problems, Pelvic, Pineal Gland Problems

Emotions

You may feel that you don't have enough support to reach out during a time of need. You may feel unworthy of being here and do not feel worthy of asking for support either. Your environment is unbalanced and out of order which is now being reflected internally. You feel that you have no plan or person to fall back on when your goals fail, almost as if you are being punished for some reason. You regret that you were not guided in a way that would enable you to make decisions on your own and take responsibility where necessary. You may feel that you are hanging in mid air and there is no reliable structure or guidance to follow. You require superior guidance that makes you feel safe. The more support you need, the more you fear you won't get it. This inevitably attracts the worst-case scenario.

Pain discussed in Volume 1.

Pancreas Problems

See Alcoholism, Cystic Fibrosis, Diabetes, Inflammation, Jaundice, Gallstones

Emotions

You often feel conquered or defeated. Hard efforts were not praise or appreciated. This made you feel rejected and triggered an old rejection trauma from childhood. This pattern that began in your childhood is still being repeated in your adult life. Your need for love may never have been met in a fulfilling way, so you are always searching for more love. You to seem feel a great emptiness, almost like a void that has no end. You also seem to feel robbed of your power and ability to stand strong against launched attacks, whether it's verbal or physical.

Influential people may have regularly rejected you, causing you to reject yourself and your goals.

Pancreatic Cancer

See Alcoholism, Cancer, Pancreas Problems

Emotions

You feel invaded by people, controlled in how you should feel and experience life. The love that was shown to you was often very conditional. You seem to feel that there is nothing out there for you. You try and find your passion and happiness outside of yourself. This often means that any feelings of fulfillment are fleeting as what you want is never within reach. Your passion for life has been squashed by a need to be in control of everything. You overcompensate for the lack of control you experienced during childhood. This typically backfires, as you are too desperate to correct past mistakes. You have given up on friends and good acquaintances, as you are not seeing any reward for the time and energy invested in other's needs and goals.

Panic Attack

See Anxiety, Alcoholism, Depression, Hyperventilation, Hysteria, Phobia, Sexual Abuse

Emotions

You have an intense fear of which the origin is often unknown. You have been over thinking and stewing on past actions and incidents. You have an unconscious fear of being punished for possible mistakes you've made. You were made to feel as a scapegoat and were treated as the root cause of everyone's problems. You often feel that it is your fault that everyone is unhappy and struggling. You accept responsibility for issues that you are unable to change. You often feel intimidated by authority figures and feel powerless in their presence. You may have to accept challenges as a result of poor boundaries, assuming you have can only suck it up, shut up and deal with it. You often feel that you are intruding on everyone's life. Everything is a mess and chaotic with no pause button.

Papillomavirus (HPV)

See under Human Papillomavirus (HPV)

Paralysis

See Brain, Paraplegia, Multiple Sclerosis, Muscle Problems, Myofascial Pain Syndrome (MPS), Nerve Problems, Spinal Cord

Emotions

You may have been blamed for causing stress in the family. This may be the result of influential people not taking responsibility for their own actions. You have accepted what was coming your way, making you overly cautious and aware of what you are doing. You are trying to avoid causing problems and recreating old mistakes that had traumatic consequences. You have stopped dead in your tracks as a result of fearing the unknown. Your actions may have been punished in the past. As a result, you are hyper vigilant about what you do and say. You were made to feel as if you were overstepping a boundary by moving outside of the family values. You want to start a new journey in life. You feel held back by controlling influential people; as if you need permission in order to change. You have learned that resisting influential people does not have a desirable outcome.

Paraplegia

See Accident, Paralysis, Spinal Cord

Emotions

Your journey has temporarily come to a halt. This condition may have surfaced just as you were about to embark on a new journey or make big new changes. You may have a deep unconscious fear of success, failure and new changes (this is related to ancestral trauma).This condition also affects your loved ones. This is a time when people will have a more in depth experience and understanding of what compassion, acceptance and forgiveness means to them. This is a condition that can turn someone's life upside down if you do not have sufficient support in your life. This condition brings about many new life experiences, for everyone involved. From what I have learned, it will trigger many unresolved issues in you and those around you.

Parasites

See Crabs, Lice, Malaria, Cercarial Dermatitis, Bacteria, Virus, Fungus, Microplasma

Emotions

Parasites in a person's body relates to people or circumstances that may be parasitic and taxing on their time and energy. Influential people only expressed love when you followed their strict instructions. You are a people pleaser, causing you to exercise poor boundaries. This is strongly linked to your lack of worthiness. You often felt you had to work and sacrifice your happiness in order to be validated and loved. People often think that parasites, bacteria and viruses are bad or evil. They are actually just a part of nature. The parasites, bacteria or viruses are doing what they are programmed to do.

Parkinson's Disease

See Muscle Problems, Myofascial Pain Syndrome (MPS), Nerve Problems, Tremor

Emotions

You are resistant to learning new information from the environment. The more you see and process, the more overwhelmed you feel. You experience life in a very sensitive way. What you have learned, seen and experienced so far is enough—you do not want to continue this emotional journey. You want to change the way you execute tasks and respond to your circumstances. There is a part of you that no longer wants to play this game called life. You are withdrawing from society as you do not want to compromise your emotional and mental health anymore. You feel rigid about what has happened in your life. You do not want to continue along that path anymore. Your stubbornness and rigidity have served you well. As a negative side effect, you suppressed your emotions. Instead, you relied on the rigidity for emotional support and comfort. You felt conflicted with your goals and what others expect of you.

Pellagra

See Alcoholism, Anxiety, Depression, Digestive Problems, Fatigue, Nerve Problems, Skin Problems, Suicide

Emotions

You feel overly sensitive to verbal attacks from others (related to ancestral trauma). You often sabotage your spiritual and emotional growth by holding on to the past. Feeling stagnant and isolated caused a great deal of anxiety. There is a deep fear of being left behind. Your environment has become emotionally and physically toxic to you. Love may have been expressed in an abusive or hostile manner. You feel that you didn't have enough nurturing and protection during childhood (related to ancestral trauma). You have been made to feel guilty for having needs, especially when you expressed yourself during times of stressful events.

Pelvic Organ Prolapsed

See Prolapsed Problems – Bladder

Pelvic Problems

See Back Problems, Bone Problems, Constipation, Female Problems, Fibromyalgia, Foot Problems, Gonorrhea, Chlamydia, Herpes, Hip Problems, Inflammation, Joint Problems, Knee Problems, Neck Problems, Male Problems, Paget's Disease, Salpingitis, Tendon Problems

Emotions

Your childhood may have been built on a foundation of instability, confusion, lack of consistency or chaos. You have been introduced to a life that may have forced you to fend for yourself early on. You may have made an association that support is not safe, not helpful or creates an opportunity for betrayal. When you needed support, how were your needs met? You had to rely on your ability to support yourself. Issues related to the pelvis may surface in many different ways. The pelvis is the foundation of the skeletal system, if this area has been injured, misaligned or damaged in any way, it may cause pain in many different areas in the body. The pelvis also relates to one's sexual relationships. It also relates to how you feel about your sexuality and bearing.

Penis Problems

See Alcoholism, Genital Warts, Gonad Problems, Infertility, Male Problems, Muscle Problems, Pineal Gland Problems, Peyronie's Disease, Premature Ejaculation, Prostate Problems, Sexual Abuse, Testosterone Problems

Emotions

You seem to have associated guilt and shame with your penis and the purpose of it. You may have been exploring this area as a child and were made to feel guilty, disgusting or ashamed. This memory may have affected you throughout your adult life, resulting in emotional and psychological issues relating to your genitals. You seem to feel uncomfortable when you are intimate with someone. You feel that you are disgusting for using this part of your body, which you made a negative association with during childhood.

Peptic Ulcer

See Bacteria, Digestive System, Ulcers

Emotions

You seem to be feeling intense anger and resentment towards an influential female figure for treating you in a way that made you feel trapped and controlled. You are suppressing intense rage as a result of not being able to speak up and feeling ignored. You seem to feel controlled by what others think. You may feel unworthy of being accepted as who you are. You have adapted to a façade that is more desirable to others. You may feel traumatized by influential people that should have protected and loved you. Instead, your needs were met by negative reactions from short-tempered influential people. You can't stomach how your mother made you feel. You need an outlet for all the intense emotions. Expressing yourself might result in more rejection and abandonment. You have associated self-expression with punishment and rejection. Silence has been a saving grace, yet it resulted in many emotions and traumas being suppressed and stewed on. Your own turmoil and emotional pain is eating away at you.

Periodontitis

See Gum Problems

Peripheral Nerve Problems

See Anxiety, Blood Pressure High, Heart Problems, Impotence Problems, Lung Problems, Muscle Problems, Nerve Problems, Spine Problems, Toxins

Emotions

You feel challenged by traumatic incidents that you are unable to express or communicate to others. Past trauma has caused you a great deal of turmoil. Life has surprised you with unexpected events and actions, leaving you feeling scared, angry or out of control. You feel suffocated by your current circumstances. This lack of expression has created a great deal of suppressed anger, to the point where it makes your blood boil. The lack of control you experienced was a result of unexpected events, behaviors and circumstances. This made you overcompensate by becoming too controlling. You still have a great need to say what should have been said in the past. These unexpressed truths have now become urgent. You may have been punished, abused or ridiculed whenever you tried to communicate. Your sensitivity to people's reactions and behavior has caused you to become disconnected from everyone.

Peyronie's Disease

See Male Problems, Muscle Problems, Penis Problems

Emotions

This is often related to a controlling, hostile or emotionally absent mother. You may feel a great need to control your partner(s), as loved ones may have abandoned you in the past. You often had to fight against abusive or manipulative parents or authority figures. You had to solely rely on your masculine qualities in order to emotionally survive, as any feminine aspects were judged and criticized.

Phantom Limb

See Accident, Anxiety, Depression, Gulf War Syndrome, Inflammation, Nerve Problems, Pain, Post-Traumatic Stress Disorder (PTSD), Spine Problems

Emotions

In some cases, people feel that they deserve to be punished for being a bad or not good enough. This often stems from a childhood that was not emotionally fulfilling. You may feel attacked by life and treated in an unfair manner. This condition may be the result of two issues. You were either controlled or you needed to be in control of everything. Your need to be overly controlling may have been the end result of being too controlled during childhood. You may now be overcompensating for the lack of control you had in the past (or the lack of control your ancestors had). There is a part of you that is expressing trauma related to an ancestor's lack of control in his or her own life.

Phobias

See Anxiety, Depression, Panic Attack

Emotions

You have experienced a trauma that caused you to develop a phobia in order to keep yourself safe, as well as not attracting the same trauma again. You have made a negative association with an activity, person, object, animal, insect or specific circumstances.

Discussed in Volume 1: Fear of flying, Fear of heights, Fear of public speaking, Fear of being outside, Fear of animals, Fear of darkness or confined spaces, Fear of dark or murky water, Fear of water

Pineal Gland Problems

See Epilepsy, Fatigue, Hypertension, Immune System, Impotence, Infertility, Insomnia, Paget's Disease, Penis Problems, Post-Traumatic Stress Disorder (PTSD), Seasonal Adjustment Disorder

Emotions

You feel a great need to belong somewhere, as though you are misplaced in life. Your trust has been betrayed and challenged by influential people. As a result, you feel unsafe and distrustful of other's intentions. You have a hard time just letting yourself "be." Feeling safe might attract unpleasant experiences, especially if you let your guard down. You were overly alert and aware of everything around you. The more you know, the safer you feel. You seem to feel challenged when you try to let go of past mistakes and unjust treatment. This pattern has a negative effect on your quality of life. You do not want to move away from what you know. You prefer to rely solely on self-acquired knowledge, as any other resources cannot be trusted.

Pinguecula

See Eye Problems - Pinguecula

Pink Eye

See Eye Problems – Conjunctivitis

Pituitary Gland Problems

See Blood Pressure High, Goiter, Graves' Disease, Hot Flushes, Hyperthyroidism, Hypothyroidism, Weight Problems

Emotions

You often take on too much and can overwhelm yourself easily. Your feminine and masculine side is out of balance. You have been emotionally scarred in life. You learned how to use your pain as a barrier/ buffer between yourself and others. Your pain helps to keep you safe. You often use anger to express personal boundaries and to push forward in life. Your ability to freely express yourself has been suppressed and tightly controlled by others who couldn't tolerate happy people. An influential person's mood dictated the mood of the household. If this influential person was unhappy, then no one else was allowed to be happy. Selfish influential people controlled you, making you feel resentful and resistant to compromise when it comes to someone else's agenda. You have a great need for freedom and independence. Your needs may have always been the last priority.

Plantar Fasciitis

See Achilles Tendon Rupture, Bone Problems, Foot Problems, Heel / Heel Spur, Inflammation, Pain

Emotions

This condition often starts during the womb stages, only to be triggered later in life when a similar stress and pressure occurs. Your mother may have felt pressured to be supportive to her partner. She may have had a challenging relationship with your father and was always on the move in order to calm her nerves. Your father was often quite stern, stubborn or controlling and this had a direct influence on how you tackled any goals and projects. You are too hard on yourself and very often sabotage your progress by overdoing certain tasks or activities with the intention of activating an adrenaline rush. You feel alive, in control and joyful when you participate in activities that distract you from old childhood blocks and/or traumas.

Plantar Warts

See Warts – Plantar Warts

Pneumonia

See Acute Interstitial Pneumonitis, Alcoholism, Auto Immune Disease, Bacteria, Fever, Fungus, Immune System Compromised, Inflammation / infection, Lung Problems, Parasites, Virus

Emotions

You feel overwhelmed by old grief, disappointment or a feeling that you being are suffocated by your emotions. In other cases, you might be in an environment where people's emotions are running high. You are very sensitive to people's behavior and reactions towards you. People and circumstances triggered your suppressed issues during a time when you felt exhausted by your own challenges. You feel helpless and powerless to change challenging circumstances. This is especially true if the client a child.

Nevertheless, even as an adult, you may find similar situations that leave you feeling powerless to change what's going on around you.

Poisoning

See Bacteria, Mercury Poisoning, Toxins

Emotions

There is something in your life that you need to get rid of. You may be in an emotionally toxic and unhealthy circumstance and/or relationship. People are causing you a great deal of stress, testing your boundaries and putting you in positions you do not want to be in. The love and attention you received from influential people may have felt toxic or poisonous. Often your need for love, security or attention was met by hostility, and/or negative attitudes from a very early age. You do not want to continue struggling anymore, you have had enough and want to block people from getting too close. You may have decided that life is full of challenges, there is no joy and what's the use.

Poliomyelitis / Polio

See Inflammation, Muscle Problems, Nerve Problems, Spine Problems, Virus

Emotions

You may feel that there is no hope of escaping the life you have. You feel frozen, as you cannot change it in any way. You may feel disheartened by life and all the doors that are closed. Desired goals are not materializing. Your circumstances have challenged you in terms of achieving your goals; they are right in front of you, but feel just out of reach. Hard work never produced any good results, so you may feel, "What is the use of all this?" You have nothing to live for or work towards and your passion or motivation has been diminished. You feel bitter as your expectations in life have not been fulfilled and you may have experienced failed relationships.

Polycystic Ovary Syndrome

See Acne, Cyst, Ovary Cancer / Problems, Depression, Diabetes, Hormone Problems, Infertility, Weight Problems

Emotions

You feel blocked when connecting to your feminine side. It is one thing to show / project it, but it's an entirely different scenario to feel it and be connected to it. You have had periods of your life when you have had to be more masculine. You were often relied on to cope with very stressful circumstances. You may have seen your mother become helpless in her life due to too many expectations and responsibilities. This may be the result of challenging relationship issues, jealousy toward a child or not being able to cope with her life.

Polyps

See Colon Problems, Lung Problems, Menstrual Problems, Sinus Problems, Uterus Problems

Emotions

You have a great need to appear strong and always be right. Your façade is strong willed and surfaces when you take on too much responsibility. You may have experienced a great loss in your life, including people leaving you unexpectedly, passing away or a relationship, which broke up, triggering old separation trauma. You seem to be stuck in the past emotionally, dealing with how certain people and circumstances made you feel. You fear letting go of the past will mean letting go of everything you hold dear. The good came with the bad and you associated positive memories with challenging and negative memories. You may feel stagnant, while everyone around you seems to be moving forward. This is the natural flow of life, yet it feels to you as if you are being abandoned and left behind.

Discussed in Volume 1: Polyps in bladder, Polyps in Cervical, Polyps in Lungs, Polyps in Nasal

Post-Laminectomy Syndrome

See Failed Back Syndrome

Post Nasal Drip

See Sinus Problems

Postpartum depression / Postnatal Depression

See Depression, Hormone Problems

Emotions

The birth process may have caused an old ancestral trauma to surface. The difference now is that you are experiencing PPD. Traumatic and new changes seem to trigger this old cycle of depression as your environment / territory has changed. Things are not the way they used to be. It is possible that your mother also suffered from this condition (it depends on the individual and how long this condition lasts). You may have been placed under a great deal of pressure to deliver a healthy child with no complications. High expectations were projected onto you (and ancestors) about how you should handle the birth.

Post-Traumatic Stress Disorder

See Adjustment Disorder, Anxiety, Attention Deficit Hyperactivity Disorder (ADHD), Depression, Gulf War Syndrome, Nervous Breakdown, Seasonal Adjustment Disorder (SAD)

Emotions

Circumstances may have threatened you; the trauma does not need to be explored in detail. What matters is how this trauma made you feel. People experience trauma differently with various levels of intensity. Whereas one person may experience PTSD during a war or military training, another person may have gone through the same experience without developing this condition. Intense trauma experienced by your ancestors may make you very sensitive towards harsh circumstances and certain behaviors of influential people. This means you will have a sensitive predisposition for certain circumstances and reactions of others. You have experienced a traumatic event and haven't completed the trauma; instead it has been suppressed. You want to escape your emotions and instead of improving your situation, you effectively make it worse. You are using a great deal of energy to keep this trauma at bay.

Pregnancy discussed in Volume 1.

See Abortion, Adoption, Birth, Eclampsia, Female Problems, Infertility, Melasma, Miscarriage, Postpartum Depression, Thyroid Problems

Premature Ejaculation

See Male Problems, Penis Problems

Emotions

You feel pressured to please a partner. Your masculinity and self-worth is connected to your sexual performance. You might be very intimidated by a partner's sexual needs. It could be that you associate sex with shame and guilt (often related to an ancestor who had sex with someone other than their partner) creating an unconscious desire to get the process over and done with. Your mother may also have wanted to have sex very quickly as it felt like an obligation or it triggered old trauma related to possible sexual abuse.

Pressure in Body discussed in Volume 1.

See Muscle Problems, Myofascial Pain Syndrome (MPS), Pelvic Problems

Prickly Heat

See Rash, Skin Problems

Emotions

You seem to have an unconscious fear of change and may be stalling in some aspect of your life. You are approaching success yet seem to be feeling irritated by the possible consequences and outcome of the new changes. You may be going through a transition and feel that your plans have been invaded or are being controlled by outside influences. You are rigid and are not flexible. As a result, you feel stuck and trapped. You have a deep need to clearly express clear boundaries and be more independent. This independence is a source of power so the more your independence is suppressed, the angrier you feel toward influential people or your circumstances.

Progeria

See Aging, Alopecia, Congenital Disorders, Depression, Eye Problems, Heart Problems, Motor Neuron Disease

Emotions

You are resistant to be part of this dysfunctional world. You are part of a family line where ancestors struggled to survive and endured a great deal of pain, trauma or depression. Your ancestors experienced countless traumas and stressful circumstances. This includes surviving in environments that may have been polluted and poisoned by toxins.

Prolapsed Problems

See Anal Problems, Digestive Problems, Colon Cancer, Intestines, Hemorrhoids, Heart Problems

Emotions

You are desperate to let go of patterns, relationships or trauma that don't serve you anymore. You seem to feel that your trauma is part of what you are made up of. Letting go of your trauma might mean that you have to let go of a part of yourself. You don't see past trauma as an experience, you feel that it is part of who you have become. In reality, trauma only influences who a person is. Your trauma is not necessarily who you are at a core level. When a person releases their trauma they are then free to become the person that they were supposed to be all along. You have experienced a great deal of loneliness and fear abandonment. Past trauma seems to feel like an old friend. You have felt rejected by others and are deeply disgusted with yourself for being so inadequate and unlikable. You are very self-conscious about how others perceive you. You feel that what others see in you will never meet your own expectations.

Prostate Cancer / Problems

See Gonads, Hormone Problems, Male Problems, Penis Problems, Testosterone Problems

Emotions

You feel blocked / held back in your creativity and spirituality. You seem to feel suppressed by a dominant partner who resembles a dominant parent from your childhood. This may also be playing out in your spiritual path. Influential people and stressful circumstances are challenging your rigidity and sense of competitiveness. This may be a direct result of a fear of abandonment, rejection or losing your purpose. It could be something that gives you importance or status.

Psoriasis

See Auto Immune Disease, Eczema, Rashes, Skin Problems

Emotions

You seem to feel pushed into circumstances that do not resonate with you. You feel that you are living someone else's life and as a result, you have completely disconnected from life. You feel trapped and controlled in your circumstances, which makes you feel powerless and manipulated by influential people. You have given your power away to all the wrong people. By playing into other people's power games, you have become afraid of rejection and abandonment. Standing your ground and expressing boundaries may result in separation. This will only trigger any old abandonment trauma.

Psychosis

See Alcoholism, Addictions – Drugs, Bipolar Disorder, Epilepsy, Hysteria, Schizophrenia, Stroke, Tumors

Emotions

Psychosis can occur as a result of prolonged drug or alcohol abuse. You have disconnected from your past and talk about it as though it doesn't matter. You have become overwhelmed by life and the responsibilities you had to deal with on your own. The more your environment triggers your old trauma, the more you suppress it. Long-term, this results in a great deal of stress, anxiety and depression. Symptoms can worsen the more denial you are in. You were not able to exercise clear boundaries as a child. As a result, you attract unhealthy, highly stressful, or abusive circumstances.

Pterigium

See Eye Problems – Pterigium

Quadriplegia

See Paraplegia

Rabies

See Nerve Problems, Virus

Emotions

You are not getting anything out of life. Your parents were controlling and possessive, making you feel suffocated with a need for permission to move forward in life. Influential people may have been protective. The protection was actually hidden hostility, jealousy or masking the need to dominate. Your parents seemed to have raised you out of obligation, resentment or expectations of influential people. You feel a great deal of anger for being on the receiving end of other's frustrations. This may include physical or verbal abuse.

Radiation

See Attack, Cancer, Poisoning, Toxin

Emotions

You have been depleted and pushed to the point of giving up. You seem to feel that life has taken everything from you and you've gotten nothing out of it. You feel angry that you have reached this stage. You are full of blame and feel that life is unfair. You have put a lot of energy and effort into helping loved ones reach their goals.

Radius

See Cumulative Trauma Disorder (known as IRS), Pain, Tendons, Wrist Problems

Emotions

You seem to be moving into a phase where you may have to give up something important in order to gain something. You often feel an obligation to a loved one and as a result, you neglect your own passion and goals. How do you feel in your work place? Explore stress related to your living environment or workplace. You feel pressured to change or adjust something that will sabotage your joy.

Rape discussed in Volume 1.

See Anxiety, Attacked, Bipolar Disorder, Hysteria, Post-Traumatic Stress Disorder (PSTD), Sexual Abuse

Rashes

See Allergies, Bacteria, Blisters, Eczema, Dermatitis, Fungus, Hives, Mercury Poisoning, Lyme Disease, Rosacea, Scarlet Fever, Seborrheic, Skin Problems

Emotions

A rash appearing on the skin is the body's way of telling you that something or someone is causing you a great deal of frustration. The rash may take many forms. It may appear as a cluster of red dots or as a large patch covering the skin. The rash can be sore, itchy, stinging or have no pain at all. Rashes come in all shapes and sizes. It can also occur anywhere on the body. Very common areas are the face, arms and back. They can also appear in the genital area, on the scalp under the hair, and across the torso. Headaches and an unspecified feeling of illness may accompany the rash.

Raynaud's Disease

See Blood Problems, Circulation Problems, Cramps, Hypoxia, Muscle Problems

Emotions

You seem to be experiencing traumas similar to what your distant ancestors experienced. They lived in extremely cold circumstances. Your ancestors felt deep anger, lack of support or love during hard and laborious hours. They may also have moved from one town to another in cold circumstances. You may be experiencing similar emotions and stress.

Reactive Arthritis discussed in Volume 1.

See Arthritis, Auto Immune Disease, Bacteria, Chlamydia, Inflammation, Joint Problems, Osteoarthritis, Rheumatoid Arthritis, Tendon Problems

Rectocele

See Prolapsed Problems – Rectal

Rectum Problems

See Anal Problems, Intestines, Genital Warts, Hemorrhoids Prolapsed Problems – Rectal

Emotions

Children experience pleasure and enjoy relieving themselves while wearing their nappies. A parent's reaction to this is often one of disgust and revulsion. You may have made a very early association that anything to do with the rectum is disgusting and shameful. You associate this area and the function of it with guilt. As time progresses, you may have learned that feces and the rectum area are dangerous and disgusting. Letting go of old food has now become a guilt trip that is filled with disgust and anger. Deep down there is a relief when you let go of old emotions along with the stool.

Reflux

See Acid Reflux, Digestive Issues, Heart Burn, Muscle Problems, Nausea

Emotions

You feel very upset, resistant or disgusted by what is going on around you. You often find yourself involved in circumstances or with people who make you to want to escape. Your overwhelming fear of loneliness and being rejected dominate all logic and make you stay in unhealthy circumstances. You sense this but are unable to fix it. You are up against too much and fear that you will fail if you keep fighting to fix everything.

Reiter's syndrome

See Auto Immune Disease, Bacteria, Inflammation / Infection, Reactive Arthritis

Renal Disease / Failure

See Kidney Problems, Uremia

Repetitive Stress Injury RSI

See Cumulative Trauma Disorder

Restless Leg Syndrome

See Anxiety, Joint Problems, Gulf War Syndrome, Muscle Problems, Myofascial Pain Syndrome (MPS), Nerve Problems, Pelvic Problems, Post-Traumatic Stress Disorder (PTSD)

Emotions

You find it challenging to connect to the part of yourself that is calm and peaceful. You may feel disconnected from others and your true self. You often work hard and are very proactive with the intention of escaping unwanted feelings and memories of childhood. You may have experienced abuse or trauma during a time when you felt safe. Stressful or threatening circumstances may have occurred unexpectedly, leaving you insecure and afraid. Incidents in the past may have left many cycles of unresolved trauma. As a result, you feel stuck in a fight or flight mode. You were at the receiving end of judgment and criticism from influential people, often taking the brunt of a parent(s) frustration.

Retina

See Eye Problems / Retina

Reye's Syndrome

See Immune System, Meningitis, Nausea, Virus

Emotions

Your desired goals are achieved with great opposition or sabotage. You seem to be a sensitive person. Ancestral trauma is now being expressed in your life along with conception trauma. You may have felt unwelcome beginning in the womb. Perhaps your mother didn't feel that she was allowed to have fun and enjoy life while she was pregnant (often related also to ancestral trauma). There were many restrictions in her life and she felt trapped as well as controlled by her circumstances. Her anger indirectly affected you in utero.

Ribs

See Bone Problems

Emotions

There is often trauma related to feeling completely exposed and unable to protect oneself.

Upper part of the ribs

Often relates to those closest to you, such as your mother or father. This could also be related to abuse that your mother or father experienced with their parents. Did someone pass away in your life that was close to you? Someone's death may have caused great upset and dysfunction in the family, having a direct affect on you.

Lower part of ribs

This relates more to your relationships (personal or work related, etc.).

Crushed ribs

May be related to feeling that your family foundation is falling apart or is not as strong as it used to be.

Rickets

See Bone Problems, Malnutrition

Emotions

Responsibility overload seems to be the key here. You may feel that you came into this world with very little support and resources. You do not have a place from which to draw your energy and life force from. Your mother may have felt this way when she was pregnant.

Rheumatism

See Back Pain, Bursitis, Inflammation, Joint Problems, Neck Pain, Pain, Rheumatoid Arthritis, Shoulder Pain

Emotions

An old trauma has been triggered after birth, when you moved from the warmth of the womb to a cold environment. This old trauma is often an ancestral trauma, where ancestors had to work and do unpleasant tasks in cold weather. Negative associations have been made with cold climate and people felt challenged by what they were doing. This could include career choices or cultural discriminations.

Rheumatoid Arthritis

See Arthritis, Attacked, Auto Immune System, Bursitis, Inflammation, Joint Problems, Osteoarthritis, Reactive Arthritis, Tendon Problems

Emotions

You only feel recognized and noticed when you accept more responsibilities. This causes a great deal of anger, as you may feel you have to work for love. You have a deep and rigid need to be right. This may be the result of feeling ignored whenever you needed to be acknowledged or heard. You feel that no one takes you seriously, which infuriates you. You have a fear of saying "no," as this may cause you to be rejected and abandoned. You tend to bend over backwards for others with very little reward. You seem to push people away, setting yourself up to endure any pain on your own.

Rosacea

See Alcoholism, Blisters, Skin Problems, Rashes

Emotions

As a child, you were taught to be seen and not heard and you have been silenced too much. You are suppressing a fierce anger that is triggered when people irritate you. You may have had a tense relationship with a parent who projected a fierce temper and sharp, hurtful words. You seem to be the one who is carrying and holding the family together. You feel responsible for everyone's happiness, success and nurturing. You push yourself too hard, as you only felt validated after working very hard. Weak efforts were punished, causing you to give too much of yourself.

Rotator Cuff Problems

See Cumulative Trauma Disorder, Joint Problems, Muscle Problems, Shoulder Problems, Tendon Problems

Emotions

You have entered a phase in life that has caused your personal and professional relationships to be out of balanced. You have taken on more responsibility and burdens. You are now becoming aware of the consequences and impact of past decisions. What was once an act of goodwill and compassion has turned into an obligation and undesired responsibility. This makes you feel angry or trapped and is taking an emotional toll. You've made a mistake by taking action on behalf of someone else but you feel too guilty to abandon the project or the person.

Rumination Syndrome

See Constipation, Depression, Diarrhea, Digestive Problems

Emotions

You seem to feel, "There is nothing and no one out there for me." The connection you shared with your mother during womb stages has been abruptly interrupted. You are more aware of all the judgment, tension or stress around them and you do not seem to bond with your mother in a way that is fulfilling. You may feel that your need for love is met by emotional absence and stress. Your needs are met by your mother's numbness or feeling challenged to express love. The love that she thinks she gave you might not be the kind of love you needed.

Rupture

See Achilles, Gonad Problems, Hernia, Muscle Problems, Tendon Problems

Emotions

You may feel that you have reached your limit. There are too many expectations and you have a deep fear of failing. Your stubbornness and resistance to give in has caused you to bite off more than you can chew. You want to accomplish the impossible, which may be the result of having to jump through hoops as a child in order to be acknowledged and loved. This is also related to patterns where you sabotage any success (often related to a fear success). You have been adding more and more stress to your life to mask the pain that you are feeling.

Sacrum

See Hip Problems - Sacrum

Salivary Gland Disorders

See Cancer, Inflammation, Mumps

Emotions

You feel and express emotions from the head mind and not from the heart or gut mind. You have experienced a trauma that made you find comfort in analyzing your circumstances instead of feeling and processing it. This has resulted in tension, pressure and unresolved trauma to become stuck in the head mind. This blocked the flow to your heart mind. This may have caused you to discard and suppress any emotions.

Salpingitis

See Fallopian Tube Problems, Infertility, Inflammation, Ovaries, Pelvic Problems, Prolapsed Problems – Uterus

Sarcoidosis

See Immune System Compromised, Inflammation, Lungs Problems, Lymphatic System

Emotions

You seem to feel consumed by suppressed grief and disappointments. Influential people have verbally attacked you because they feel you are not good enough. You have failed to become the ideal person that authority figures pushed you to become. You long for acceptance just for being yourself. Your self-esteem is motivated by your efforts and hard work, which never seem to be enough. Your opinions and efforts were often ignored, leaving you to feel unworthy and unable to feel like an equal in the family.

Scabies

See Skin Problems, Eczema, Parasites

Emotions

You seem to feel irritated and invaded by those that are overstepping your boundaries. You do not feel worthy enough to say "no." You often feel challenged when confronted by disrespectful people. You have a fear that if you do say "no," you will be rejected and end up alone and abandoned. People are taking advantage of your poor boundaries, causing a great deal of stress and inner conflict. Your fear of rejection is holding you back. You know that your boundaries are being overstepped however, you feel powerless to do something about it. As a result, you feel very irritated and aggravated by these people.

Scarlet Fever

See Bacteria, Fever, Heart Problems, Lymphatic System, Strep Throat, Toxins

Emotions

There seems to be a strong pattern in the family where verbal attacks and unnecessary accusations were thrown back and forth. You walked right into the middle of a blame throwing tug of war between two influential people. You never seem to know when it will be your turn to be attacked, blamed or made to feel guilty and ashamed for being in the wrong place at the wrong time. Influential people failed to take responsibility for their mistakes and decisions. You feel burdened by the blame game and very misunderstood as no one can focus on your needs.

Schizophrenia

See Addictions, Bi-polar Disorder, Catalepsy, Depression, Epilepsy, Hyperactivity, Hysteria, Panic Attack, Psychosis

Emotions

When you witness or have met someone with schizophrenia, it becomes quite evident that they behave and think in a scattered way. They have ideas and words coming from all directions and different thoughts and feelings coming and going in waves. They suffer from false beliefs such as thinking they are being chased or are under attack. As a schizophrenic, you may feel that uncontrollable forces are controlling you. You often lead a lonely life as you avoid being around people who could be a potential threat. You may hear voices and can even sometimes experience senses such as taste, smell or even see things that are not real. You do not trust in the world and your environment. You cannot count on what is real and what is not, as you feel deceived by your own reality.

Sciatica Nerve

See Back Problems, Hip Problems, Nerve Problems, Pain, Peripheral Nerve

Emotions

You have felt emotionally and physically invaded by your family. Your boundaries and right to privacy have not been respected. You feel humiliated, belittled or disconnected from your territory, family and identity. You often accept the role of scapegoat in the family because you feel you have no right to speak up for or defend yourself. You feel manipulated into going through with something you don't want to participate in but feel you lack the coping skills to fight back. Your ideas and opinions are communicated in a way that is not understood by others. This causes you a great deal of tension and imbalance, often leading to isolation. Communication is very important to you, yet you continually feel misunderstood. You have a lot to share and express, yet unspoken words have accumulated without an outlet creating anger and rage.

Sclerosis

See Back Problems, Multiple Sclerosis, Muscle Problems, Pain

Scoliosis

See Back Problems, Hip Problems, Muscle Problems, Osteoporosis, Pain, Skeletal System, Spine Problems

Emotions

You have been suppressed by dominant, controlling influential people who used guilt, threats or shame in order to control your behavior. Your need for approval was met by comments such as "You can do better than that" or "That is acceptable, but not good enough." You seem to feel that your efforts and hard work were never good enough. The harder you worked, the more judgment and criticism you attracted. You have associated success and handwork with humiliation or lack of reward. You were caught between your mother and father's conflict. They may have been given the ultimatum to choose between them. Problems and complaints were also dumped on you, making you feel overwhelmed and stressed. You often had no idea who to please and who to push away. Either way, you were in the firing line of your parent's conflict. Rigid, influential people controlled your future and made personal choices on your behalf.

Seasonal Adjustment Disorder (SAD)

See Adjustment Disorder, Anxiety, Depression, Nervous Breakdown, Sleep Problems

Emotions

You may have experienced an unpleasant phase in life during a certain season. As a result, you have made negative associations with the season during which you experienced a trauma.

When that time of the year approaches, it may trigger the unresolved trauma(s). You feel tired, fatigued and moody. You may be suffering from depression. The fatigue is a secondary symptom and is a result of trying to escape old unresolved traumas that are surfacing in your relationships or career. The trauma may have occurred at an early stage in your life or you may be experiencing trauma related to ancestors who had to endure harsh circumstances during a specific season.

Sebaceous Cyst (Epidermal)

See Acne, Auto Immune Disease, Cyst, Skin Problems

Emotions

You have allowed yourself to be pushed and dominated into a corner. You have given your power away to an influential person. This person has triggered your childhood trauma. This influential person is mirroring a dominant figure that challenged you during childhood (or a person that challenged your mother). This cycle reinforces a victim state in which you have become stuck. You feel destined for hardship or abuse. You are snowed under by responsibilities and feel responsible for another's failures. This is a result of a domineering parent who blamed or manipulated you as a means of control. Your parents may have avoided taking responsibility for their role as a parent and avoided their own problems and shortcomings by holding you responsible for everything that didn't work out for them.

Seizures

See Epilepsy

Senility

See Addictions, Alcoholism, Alzheimer's Disease, Anxiety, Dementia, Malnutrition, Multiple Sclerosis, Panic Attacks, Parkinson's Disease, Poisoning, Thyroid Problems, Toxins, Tumors

Emotions

You have "packed up" and given up trying to change your life. You had to take care of too many responsibilities and problems during childhood. This caused you to associate life with only burdens—no joy, no support and no understanding. You may have felt unwelcomed and unwanted from an early age. You often felt punished with chores and responsibilities that gave you no joy.

Septicemia

See Bacteria, Blood Problems, Fever, Immune System Impaired, Inflammation, Poisoning, Toxins

Emotions

You feel betrayed by the people you confided in. You feel intimated by your circumstances, which made you more sensitive to verbal attacks, betrayal or feeling out of control. You feel intense anger and resentment as a result of a situation that has grown out of hand. Your anger and resentment has no outlet because you have suppressed emotions far too long. You have reached a point where you need to deal with unresolved issues and feelings. You often overact as a result of pent up anger and feeling done in by people you trusted.

Sexual Abuse discussed in Volume 1.

See Addiction, Alcoholism, Anxiety, Attacked, Bladder Problems, Bi-polar Disorder, Bulimia, Depression, Fibromyalgia, Irritable Bowel Syndrome, Lower Back Pain, Panic Attacks, Pelvic Problems, Prolapsed Problems / Uterus, Rape

Shingles

See Chicken Pox, Immune System, Nerve Problems, Rashes, Skin Problems, Spinal Cord, Virus

Emotions

You often feel overburdened by life and are carrying everyone's problems on your back, especially those of your mother or father's. The bond between you and your parents may have been hostile and cold. The parents may have been physically present, yet emotionally absent. You may have been made to feel that your efforts were never good enough when trying to please either of your parents. This is a pattern that your mother or father most likely experienced with their own parents. You were made to feel ashamed and guilty for expressing your emotions. This resulted in deep-seated resentment, as you felt suppressed by influential people. You feel that a dominant influential person controlled and dominated your journey and future, which you had no control over or say in the matter.

Shin Splits

See Bone Problems, Joint Problems, Muscle Problems, Myofascial Pain Syndrome, Tendon Problems

Emotions

You do not want others to see your weaknesses. You also do not want your true personality to shine. You have a fear of being humiliated, belittled, devalued or rejected. Being yourself makes you feel vulnerable and exposed. This causes you to feel unable to control how others see and respond to you. You feel weak when you are yourself and for this reason, you often push people away. Failure is not an option and you tend to place immense pressure on yourself to achieve your goals. You may have made a mistake in the past and are now overcompensating so as not to make the same mistake(s) again. You may feel unsupported in what you do. Your circumstances have been challenging and hostile. Your life has been bitter sweet so far; the good times always seem to be accompanied by the bad times.

Shoulder Problems

See Accidents, Back Problems, Calcification, Cumulative Trauma Disorder, Frozen Shoulder, Muscle Problems, Myofascial Pain Syndrome (MPS), Neck Problems, Rotator Cuff Problems, Tendon Problems

Emotions

You feel weighed down by responsibilities, yet are still willing to take on more. Your value is measured by how much you can do for others. You do not trust others to pull through for you or support you. Instead, you prefer to support others, as you are able to control the outcome of a task or responsibility. This makes you feel that you have to do everything by yourself in order to get it done right. Taking on responsibilities is not what gives you the fulfillment you crave such as love, acceptance or praise.

However, it's the gate to being accepted.

Sickle Cell

See Anemia, Arthritis, Blood Problems, Malaria, Urinary Infection, Virus

Emotions

You do not allow love to flow into your life. You avoid receiving love fearing that it will be accompanied by conditions and burdens. You have made a negative association with love from any early age. You feel deeply unworthy of being loved and accepted. Your self-loathing has caused you to cut yourself off from the family. You are exhausted by always trying to keep the peace. You find security in your sleeping patterns, as this is the only time when you can escape from reality.

Silicosis

See Asthma, Lung Problems

Emotions

You are storing a great deal of suppressed and unprocessed grief in the lungs (often related to ancestral trauma). This could possibly stem from a stressful and fear based childhood where one parent was the victim of abuse. As a result, you may have suffered as well. You may have felt unprotected by influential people who were not able to defend themselves. Influential people didn't always responded to your need for security. You often suppress how you feel. Expressing yourself in the past often attracted rejection and ridicule. You may have felt restricted and trapped in your past circumstances. Your future feels controlled and restricted by a lack of resources and confidence. You may feel that you can never be as good as the next person. This causes you to take and accept whatever opportunity you can find, even if it means abandoning you own goals. You feel emotionally restricted as influential people controlled you during childhood.

Sinus Problems / Sinusitis

See Allergies, Flu, Inflammation, Head Ache, Maxillary Sinus, Migraine, Polyps

Emotions

You seem to be suppressing a great deal of irritation. You feel offended by a smell in your environment that is triggering old childhood trauma. Your circumstances are draining and you see no reward as a result of your hard work. You do not want to stay where you are, but you don't feel worthy of speaking up and voicing how you feel. Instead, you suppress your emotions and truth. As a result, you feel isolated, lonely and unloved. You are searching for love and seem to feel that you will never find it. You may be going through a phase where you are reflecting on the past. You do not allow yourself to enjoy life along with others. You disconnect and punish yourself by pushing away the people who love you. You may have made a negative association with love and feel offended or threatened when love is shown. You often make everyday experiences harder and more challenging by blocking support that is offered to you. This is a result of a self-punishing habit.

Skeletal System

See Accident, Back Problems, Bone Problems, Bone Cancer, Concussion, Osteoporosis, Scoliosis

Emotions

You seem to feel deep resentment toward someone or circumstances. Your resentment is eating away at you, right to the bone. It's a deep-seated anger that is often brought on by your fear of communication. You do not communicate your need for protection. Your emotions are all over the place because you have never been given a clear structure and or guideline to follow on how to behave and communicate. The foundation and structure that your life was built on is slowly but surely giving way and you do not have the coping "tools" to fix or amend it. You often feel stuck in your circumstances. You feel stripped of your support. This caused you to feel a great deal of anger and resentment as you feel helpless and unsure of how to change any undesirable circumstances.

Skin Cancer

See Cancer, Melanoma, Skin Problems, Rashes, Toxins

Skin Problems

See Acne, Athlete's Foot, Bacteria, Blisters, Eczema, Fungus, Hives, Mastocytosis, Mercury Poisoning, Psoriasis, Rashes, Rosacea, Dermatitis, Shingles, Vitiligo, Warts

Emotions

The skin is the barrier between a person and the world. Deep seated insecurities and irritations can surface on the skin if a person is irritated or triggered. The skin is a person's physical boundary and it keeps them safe and protected. When circumstances, environmental factors or people challenge this barrier, it will speak up for itself by means of itching, burning or feeling irritated. The skin will let a person know that a physical or emotional boundary has been overstepped. When their boundaries are challenged, it can result in the person feeling inadequate, unworthy to say "no" and express boundaries when needed.

Sleep Apnea

See Apnea

Sleep Disorders General

See Anemia, Apnea, Narcolepsy, Fatigue, Insomnia, Seasonal Adjustment Disorder

Emotions

You often feel incomplete with your life and you do not understand the origin of your problems, blocks and issues. You seem to be trying to fix the symptom of your problem by sleeping. In most cases, you are experiencing a range of emotions that have been triggered by your environment and influential people. These issues arise from ancestral and in utero trauma. These types of trauma make it more challenging for you to identify the origin of the issue.

Slipped Disc

See Back Problems, Pain, Spinal Cord Problems

Emotions

You have overloaded yourself with other people's problems. You are now wondering whether you can cope with this extra load of responsibilities and stress. There has been an overlap between your responsibilities and someone else's responsibilities. You feel a deep need to be supported and loved, hence your support of other people. What you have given to others is what you actually need yourself. You are denying yourself the love and support that you deserve. You were made to feel unworthy of asking for support and love. Influential people were emotionally unavailable, possibly leaving you to your own defenses. As a result, you feel a great deal of anger and resentment for being abandoned when you should have been supported. You have experienced a similar trauma in your present life that triggered an unresolved childhood trauma related to your challenged relationship with authority figures (this could be a father figure).

Small Intestine

See Intestine – Small

Smoking

See Addictions, Emphysema, Lung Problems

Emotions

You had too many responsibilities during childhood that caused you to have to support and fend for yourself. You may have emotionally supported the family, feeling from an early age that you were obligated to step into that role. You need to calm your mind from stress and circumstances that you cannot control. Poor personal boundaries seem to be a problem for you. You feel disgusted with yourself but find running away from you problems is more appealing than dealing with them. You often use your habit of smoking to suppress a need to fight and escape from deep-seated anger and circumstances that you cannot escape. You have felt a loss of masculine power. It did not feel safe to explore and exercise your masculine qualities during your adolescent years. Key words are loss of power and respect. Smoking also creates a barrier around you to ward off people from entering your personal space. There may have been peer pressure and a need to be accepted when you smoked for the first time.

Sneezing

See Allergy

Emotions

You feel invaded by someone (loss of territory or feeling unable to control your environment). You feel that people are stronger than you are which makes you feel powerless. What were you thinking of or what was said when you sneezed? Often you will have a stress or trauma related to it. You feel stuck in circumstances and feel unsupported or unable to make a decision.

Snoring

See Apnea, Fatigue, Lungs Problems

Emotions

Snoring is often related to someone who has stopped looking after his or her health and fitness. They have begun to neglect their own needs. They may not be as active as they used to be. The muscles in the airway may have weakened as the person becomes less activate. You may have become lazier in certain aspects of your life. You have disconnected from your passion due to worthiness blocks. You may have a fear of being more successful than others. You have seen others being punished for their hard work and success causing you to fear that ...cks and criticisms.

yofascial Pain Syndrome (MPS)

Stuttering, Tic

people. You fear being interrupted when you
e of what you need to express might be missed or
e been punished for saying the wrong thing to the
ve associated trauma with communication, whether
just having a conversation. This may be related to
uld not deliver a message quick enough and this

ems, Cumulative Trauma Disorder, Herpes,
Scoliosis, Skeletal System, Slipped Disc

ed or dominated in your life. You refuse to give in to
of others. You've learned from experience that
e short end of the rope. You have a fear of being
u may also have a fear of success and feel utterly
ot to be more successful than a dominant authority
nd and being small kept you out of harm's way. You
sulting in self-sabotage. You seem to feel unworthy
n made to feel guilty and ashamed by an influential
past.

See Back ... blems

Emotions

You experienced a trauma that left you feeling abandoned, rejected or unsupported both emotionally and financially. You may have been controlled, bullied or dominated by influential people or a person that had little regard for your needs. You seem to feel that you have nowhere to turn for support, as those who can support you are emotionally unavailable or made you feel guilty for expressing needs.

Spinal Stenosis

See Arthritis, Back Problems, Nerve Problems, Kennedy's Disease, Pain, Rheumatoid Arthritis

Spleen Problems

See Bacteria, Inflammation / Infection

Emotions

You may have associated love with trauma. As a result, you became confused about what love is and should feel like. You may feel confused as to how love should be expressed. The way that love may have been shown to you caused you to feel guilty, ashamed or rejected. You have a deep need for love, yet as a result of the negative associations made, you often reject it. You feel attacked and abused by influential people that should have loved and protected you.

Sprain

See Accident, Inflammation, Muscle Problems, Pain, Tendon Problems

Emotions

You seem to feel out of control and unable to regain enough control to feel safe in your personal or professional life. You gave your power away and now feel suppressed by dominant individuals who challenge your self worth and limit your future. You often feel indecisive, not knowing what you want to do with your life. There was a lack of guidance from those whose opinions you trust and value. You feel out of control and are overcompensating by being overly rigid and stubborn about choices you make. You have become judgmental and resentful toward the people who caused you to doubt yourself.

Stigmatism

See Astigmatism, Eye Problems

Stomach Cancer

See Cancer, Inflammation, Stomach Problems, Ulcers

Emotions

You feel a great deal of anger that you are not able to process and let go of. Your emotions have become very intense and you are trying to control your feelings toward a person or circumstances. The more you communicate your disgust, anger or disapproval, the more confrontation you attract / provoke. You found yourself in a circumstance from which you could not escape. You felt a great deal of resistance toward someone or something in your life that challenged your goals or relationships. Mistakes made in the past have now come back to haunt you. Certain people or situations are a constant reminder of the poor decisions you have made. You feel unable to escape the emotional consequences of your past.

Stomach Fat

See Muscle Problems, Weight Problems

Emotions

This is often related to emotional abuse, rejection or always feeling criticized. You want to retreat and hide from an influential person. You are longing for comfort and safety and feel unprotected or lack sufficient insulation from harsh words. If you are female then explore any trauma related to the loss of a baby. Trauma related to not being able to conceive. Issues relating to regret in these areas or feeling rejected by your children. If you are a mother then this could also be related to your children changing, growing up, and moving on with their own lives. You may not feel needed anymore, even though you still want to be needed. Your self-worth and value in life is associated with being needed and helping others.

Stomach Problems

See Irritable Bowel Syndrome, Digestive Problems Colon Cancer, Candida, Hernia, Intestines

Emotions

You feel obligated to accept the families' emotional burdens. This is a result of feeling obligated to make up for being a bad person or for causing problems. The family did not exercise healthy boundaries. One person's problem was everyone else's problem and those who did not suffer along with the rest, were considered unsupportive and were punished or isolated. You were not allowed to cry. You have developed a survival instinct to lay low, (hiding instinct). You never knew when the next emotional outburst was going strike. The body is always ready to fight or flight and as a result, it might produce too much gastric acid. This is also related to the vomiting instinct. The body tries to rid itself of excess acid and get away from it or discharge it. This often relates to a person who is trying to rid themselves of circumstances that are triggering old traumas. It's the body's way of trying to create a barrier between the person and their stressful environment.

Strep Throat

See Bacteria, Fever, Inflammation, Scarlet Fever, Throat Problems

Emotions

You feel angry for not being able to express or defend yourself whenever you're confronted. You felt under attack (either verbally or physically) by people who resent you and feel threatened by you. You may have felt unfairly blamed during childhood as a result of influential people's mistakes and shortcomings. You were on the receiving end of people's pent up anger and frustration. You seem to feel punished for being yourself. You are scared of saying what needs to be said. You felt verbally attacked by influential people when you expressed yourself, causing you a great deal of sadness. You were not able to speak up and be heard. This has made you feel worthless and unworthy of being heard and acknowledged. You want to jump up and down to be noticed and acknowledged!

Stroke

See Blood Pressure (High), Blood Problems, Hemorrhoids, Tremor

Emotions

You want to be loved but at the same time, have an unconscious fear of receiving love. You have made negative associations with love. Receiving love may have caused you to feel out of control. When you needed love during childhood, your parents were often frustrated or out of control. Now you may have a fear of love and losing control of your own life. This has caused many self-sabotaging patterns. This fear has reflected itself throughout your relationships and interactions with people. This cycle has now come full circle. Your emotions have become intense and overwhelming over time—it is almost literally paralyzing you. Love has a very dark side and you know how much it can hurt if you allow yourself to become vulnerable. You have invested a great deal of energy protecting yourself from love that may potentially harm, expose or weaken you. You feel mentally and emotionally challenged whenever you communicate the need for more control, love, safety or affection. The way in which you expressed your emotional needs was not always understood. This made you feel unloved, unfulfilled or ignored.

Stuttering

See Learning Disability, Muscle Problems, Speech, Tic
Emotions
You are fearful of expressing your honest opinion. You don't want to voice your needs. Your problems are magnified when you are around people who are very vocal in conversation. You may feel forced to communicate in a way that doesn't resonate with you. You are often sensitive people in a harsh family. Harsh communication may have been projected at you while you expressed yourself. When I refer to "harsh communication" bear in mind that what is harsh to you might not be harsh to someone else. Keep an open mind. You experienced a trauma when you communicated, which resulted in a fight, flee or freeze response. Now when you communicate, it automatically triggers the old childhood trauma. This results in the gut instinct being activated. This will have a direct impact on how fluently you communicate to others.

Suicide discussed in Volume 1.

See HIV, Anxiety, Attacked, Catalepsy, Depression, Gulf War Trauma, Mercury Poisoning

Sweating

See Fever, Gland Problems, Inflammation, Mercury Poisoning, Poisoning, Toxins
Emotions
This condition relates to excessive sweating without exercise being the cause. You are stuck in a panic mode. This is often very subtle however; it's an ongoing emotional state. Sweating is increased when you are feeling emotionally trapped, panicked or anxious about a situation that you cannot control. It's as if you are trying to control an invisible force in your life.

Syphilis

See Bacteria, Dementia, Yaws
Emotions
You feel a great deal of shame and guilt related to your sexuality. You were made to feel that your self-worth is dependent on how you express your sexuality. You may have been raised with conflicting values in regard to sexuality and how one should express it. You feel guilty

for expressing yourself through sexuality. You felt approved of and accepted when you complied with others needs and demands, regardless how it made you feel.

Teeth Problems

See Bacteria, Bone Problems, Bulimia, Hypophosphatasia, Inflammation / Infection, Mercury Poisoning (as result of tooth fillings), Malnutrition

Emotions

You seem to feel stuck in a time lapse. You feel resistant to move forward in life and away from debilitating and self-sabotaging patterns. You are depriving yourself of joy, happiness and fun. You feel that others are always more entitled to have fun and express themselves freely. Your self-worth strongly relates to the amount of approval your mother or father gave you.

Teeth Grinding

See Temporomandibular Joint and Muscle Disorder (TMJD) Jaw Grinding / Clenching

Temples

See Migraine, Temporomandibular Joint and Muscle Disorder (TMJD)

Emotions

You are fighting against your environment and issues you cannot control. You also seem to be avoiding confrontational people that are placing a great deal of pressure on you. You often jump the gun and get involved with circumstances before the time is right. As a result, you feel out of sync with life, as if things are working against you.

Temporomandibular Joint and Muscle Disorder (TMJD)

See Allergies, Anxiety, Headache, Hearing Impairment, Muscle Problems, Myofascial Pain Syndrome (MPS), Parasites, Tendon Problems, Tinnitus

Emotions

If the grinding or clenching is caused by allergies then the body is feeling invaded, attacked or irritated due to its reaction to a substance from its environment. The allergic reaction may trigger unconscious feelings such as needing to get away or escape from someone; feeling irritated and trapped without an option or way to change it. You may feel imposed upon, causing anger and frustration. You have suppressed a great deal of emotions and words. It stems from a time when you were forced to listen to and obey influential people. There may be incidents where this type of trauma has been associated with physical or sexual abuse. You are stewing over old trauma you are too scared to face in your waking life.

Tendonitis

See Tendon Problems

Tendon Problems

See Achilles, Arthritis, Cramps, Cumulative Trauma Disorder, Bursitis, Foot Problems, Inflammation, Joint Problems, Muscle problems, Osteoarthritis, Reactive Arthritis, Rupture

Emotions

You may not have had enough space to move around in the womb. This is a result of a lack of space or not moving around enough. This may have resulted in different parts of the body feeling stuck in painful and uncomfortable positions. This may have been the starting point of stress and tension that was placed on the tendons. If you didn't have enough space to move around in the womb, ask yourself, "How did that make me feel?" The answer you find could often be the same issue that always arises when you are experiencing the tendon problems. It's important to find the emotional association made when you had the tendon problem. The answer that you are searching for should not be a superficial answer. You are searching for a much deeper answer.

Tennis Elbow

See Elbow Problems, Cumulative Trauma Disorder, Inflammation, Joint Problems, Muscle Problems, Tendon Problems

Emotions

You may have stretched yourself too far physically or emotionally in life. You seem to be in a situation where you feel you are losing control. You are bored and tired of the same old routine. You feel obligated to provide and support loved ones. As a result, you prioritize everyone else's needs before your own. Your happiness is drawn from other people's happiness. It is time for you to move into a role where you can attend to your own needs and find a balance between giving and receiving.

Testicle Problems

See Male Problems, Penis Problems, Prostate Problems

Emotions

You do not feel safe and comfortable expressing your sexuality. It is not safe to be masculine or feminine without provoking confrontation, judgment, rejection or abandonment. You seem to feel worthless being a male figure and feel challenged finding balance in your life. This includes when to be in control of the masculine side and when to be more feminine. There seems to be confusion—when to be relaxed and when to take action. You may question your ability to be successful on your own. Responsibilities in your life may have been taken care of on your behalf during childhood. As a result, you may problem solve in a way that is stressful and filled with sabotage because you lack guidance. You have no clear starting point for being independent. This example could also be to the other extreme where you had to take care of everything for everyone during your childhood.

Testosterone Problems

See Gonads, Male Problems, Penis Problems, Prostate Problems

Emotions

You feel unable to draw any power from your masculinity. You often find it challenging to express yourself in a way that would enable others to understand your opinions and needs.

You may have been made to feel ashamed of your masculinity or told that it's dangerous, abusive or weak. Ancestral trauma related to hard and strenuous labor and slavery. They were in circumstances that required them to be hard, aggressive and even abusive in order to survive.

Throat Problems

See Larynx Cancer, Muscle Problems, Thyroid Problems

Emotions

You feel rejected in your personal relationships. This made you suppress your truth until it has become pressing and urgent. You feel restricted in many aspects of your life. As a result, the pressure, anger and grief have built up in the throat area. You have had enough of being silenced by influential people. In childhood, your words were cut off mid sentence—you were never allowed to complete what you needed to say. You want to speak up, however you seem to attract hostile circumstances whenever you do. You often find it challenging to express any sadness or to cry. You are suppressing sadness and holding back tears. You have poor personal boundaries. When you did communicate boundaries, you often experienced rejection. As a result, you suppress your truth when confronted with challenging people and circumstances.

Thrombosis

See Blood Clot, Blood Problems, Circulation Problems, Heart Problems, Varicose Veins

Thrush

See Bacteria, Candida – Thrush in mouth, Fungus, Vaginitis

Thymus Problems

See Muscle Problems, Throat Problems

Emotions

You were made to feel that your identity is dirty in some way. Influential people, who were battling with their own self-loathing issues, projected their insecurities onto you. You do not attend to your own needs, as there was always something more important to deal with. You would much rather support others instead of being supported. You feel out of control when you are supported because being supported made you feel weak, incompetent and it challenged your need to be in control. You do not express your needs and appropriate boundaries when you are supported. You feel safer to sabotage the support, as you are then able to take control again.

Thyroid Problems

See Grave's Disease, Hashimoto's Disease, Hyperthyroidism, Hypothyroidism, Pituitary Gland Problems

Emotions

You have a deep fear of not being heard and being misunderstood so you communicate your opinions with great urgency. You fear that you will not have enough time to say what needs to be said. You invest a great deal of energy making sure that you are understood. You have a deep unconscious fear of being attacked if your intentions are misinterpreted. You feel undermined and attacked by those who should have listened and protected you. Instead, you felt attacked and threatened in your own territory. This left you feeling that nowhere is safe. You also seem to have a fear of not receiving your fair share of love and acknowledgement. This can often makes you become aggressive with the intention of making sure that you receive the acknowledgement and love you deserve. Aggression = respect, being heard and safety.

Tic (involuntary movements of muscles)

See Abasia, Chorea, Cramps, Duchenne muscular dystrophy, Dystonia, Huntington's Disease, Muscle Problems, Myofascial Pain Syndrome (MPS), Stroke
Emotions
You may have experienced trauma and shock during infancy stages that may not have been resolved by the body. As your life has progressed, you may have experienced another unrelated trauma that served as the final trigger of this condition. You felt challenged to act out a desired movement or behavior during a moment of trauma. This could include needing to escape and run away, yet for whatever reason you could not escape. The memory of the unresolved trauma remains in your legs and unconscious mind. This is an ancestral trauma that has been triggered. You might have spasms or jerking reactions in your legs as the body is still trying to resolve the trauma. This may also be the result of emotional trauma where you felt like running away but couldn't. As a result, you are stuck in a conflicting flight or fight trauma. You are dealing with a great deal of anger and frustration while trying to regain control of your life.

Tinea Capitis

See Alopecia, Hair Loss / Problems, Kerion Celsi, Parasites, Rashes, Skin Problems
Emotions
You feel attacked, invaded, controlled and punished for being related to a culture or family that has been under scrutiny. Your identity may have caused you a great deal of stress, abuse, rejection or abandonment. You do not seem to feel safe in your environment and may have been exposed to a family that was very critical, hostile or angry. Mistakes were not tolerated. You have been caught up in the middle of disputes. You have also been made to feel guilty and ashamed for being the cause of disputes even though you had no direct involvement. You seem to feel unprotected, as the sources that should protect you can't even protect themselves.

Tinnitus

See Anxiety, Hearing Impairment, Meniere's Disease, Migraine, Temporomandibular Joint and Muscle Disorder (TMJD)
Emotions
In most cases tinnitus is related to a person that is fed-up with their living arrangements / working conditions or immediate environment. You may feel obligated to listen to someone for whom you have lost respect due to their abusive characteristics (when I say abusive, it can range from very small incidents to severe cases. Abuse does not always necessarily have to be

severe. It depends how you respond to the abuse). It all boils down to feeling like you have to just take it. Now you are ready to walk away from it all, but feel held back by fear. You do not feel that you have the inner strength to stand up for yourself. Inevitably, you become a victim of your own poor boundaries.

Example of a woman who suffered from tinnitus: She was breaking-up with her husband. He was verbally abusive to her during that time. She knew that they were going to separate. She created a barrier between her and her husband due to the anger and resentment that pushed her beyond her limits. She stopped listening to his insults. At the same time, she stopped listening to herself. She overcompensated by cutting herself off from everything, including herself. She stopped listening to her own needs and judgment.

You have been under a great deal of pressure in your life. The circumstances that caused you to feel under pressure changed, creating less stress and emotional or even physical pressure. It begs the question, "Where in your life have you been under pressure and then the pressure suddenly changed?"

Toes

See Foot Problems

Emotions

General remarks: Self-punishment and feeling unworthy of what you are working toward. Fear related to inability to control the outcome and manifestation of your power. You may have been punished or undermined by influential people with the intention of keeping yourself small and controlled. You have a fear of losing control and balance in your life.

Tongue Problems

See Allergies, Candida, Nerve Problems, Muscle Problems, Stutter

Emotions

You may be feeling a great deal of humiliation related to the ancestry line. You have an unconscious fear that if you had to speak up you would be humiliated or punished. Your truth was not acknowledged as a child and as a result, you do not feel worthy of other people's time and support. You have internalized a great deal of anger and taken it out on those you felt comfortable speaking with (loved ones). You often silently blame others for your circumstances.

Tonsil Problems / Tonsillitis

See Bacteria, Inflammation / Infection, Parasites, Strep Throat, Throat Problems, Virus

Emotions

You were controlled by means of shame and being blamed by influential people. You are feeling intense emotions such as sadness, resentment, confusion or needing more love from an influential person. You are questioning your judgment and feel stuck in limbo, "Should I or shouldn't I speak? Should I ask for more love or will I be punished?" You tend to act or speak first and then think. This pattern only attracted punishment and awkward circumstances. You do not feel safe enough to be yourself and instead suppress your talents as you may have been attacked or criticized. The more you allow yourself to shine, the more vulnerable and exposed you feel. You do not allow yourself to speak up or ask for any needs to be met.

Tourette Syndrome

See Dystonia, Muscle Problems, Tic

Toxins

See Asbestos, Attacked, Cirrhosis, Immune System, Lead Poisoning, Mercury Poisoning, Poisoning, Septicemia, Tremor

Emotions

You feel under attack (mentally, verbally, emotionally and spiritually). You often overact towards your environment due to pre-existing issues that have taken a toll on you. This may stem from a childhood that was filled with dramatic, hostile and unpredictable moods or circumstances. The family may have said one thing and meant something else. This left you feeling a great deal of anxiety, as you never quite understood what was expected of you. The only way of life that you knew was filled with stress, anxiety or feeling invaded. Influential people have invaded your values and boundaries.

Tremor

See Abasia, Addictions, Chorea, Concussion, Cramps, Duchenne muscular dystrophy, Dystonia, Fatigue, Huntington's Disease, Malnutrition, Mercury Poisoning, Multiple Sclerosis, Muscle Problems, Parkinson's Disease, Stroke, Tic, Toxins

Emotions

You seem to have a deep need to start over and move away from everything that you once knew. You want to break free from old habits and patterns. You are stuck due to a fear of the future and the possible consequences if you did make a change. You may have been told that by staying where you are, you will be safe. If you move, it could lead to danger. You feel conflicted by what you've been told, what you have learned and what you really want.

Trigeminal Neuralgia

See Acoustic Neuroma, Bell's Palsy, Circulation Problems, Nerve Problems, Neuralgia, Pain

Emotions

You felt invaded or violated and lacked privacy as a result of an invasive family (you could also be expressing ancestral trauma related to this). The family may not have had proper discernment in regard to boundaries (expressing it, recognizing it and respecting it), especially when it came to your boundaries. What you have to say is not acknowledged. A controlling parent that had limited discernment of other people's emotions and feelings has twisted your truth. You lacked the support you needed from your family members and grew up in a hostile environment. You felt under attack and had to fight for your right to privacy and freedom. You were made to feel ashamed for expressing boundaries.

Tuberculosis

See Bacteria, Fever, Inflammation / Infection, Lung Problems, Pain

Emotions

You may feel that you have not been given a chance to make it out there on your own. You feel held back by influential people and your circumstances. You are in a position where you cannot speak up and feel you cannot make the necessary changes to your lifestyle. You feel like a victim of circumstance and feel hopeless, powerless or directionless. There is a deep feeling that this is not fair, as if you are being attacked for no valid reason. You are holding others accountable for your suffering. You have been stuck in a self-punishing cycle. Your life has been full of challenges. You seem to believe that you deserve nothing better than what you have already achieved. You are stubborn, rigid or inflexible. Life has been your enemy and you have felt rejected by it right from the beginning. You have experienced a "hardening of the attitude" and feel angry and upset with everything that has caused you any upset or challenges.

Tumor

See Acoustic Neuroma, Cancer, Cyst, Kaposi Sarcoma, Lipoma

Emotions

You tend to sabotage many aspects of your life. The self-sabotage seems to be driven by a feeling that you don't deserve the good things in life. You may have realized that you are admired and appreciated only when you put yourself through a great deal of hardships and challenges. You feel recognized through your pain. You may be experiencing the same self-sabotaging patterns as your parents. This includes feeling angry and resentful of others who are living the life that you want. As a result, you do not trust your own judgment or the intentions of others. You made a negative and even traumatic association with trust.

Ulcers

See Bleeding, Inflammation, Canker Sores, Blisters, Peptic Ulcer

Emotions

You have been suppressing strong emotions related to hatred / anger, vengeance, betrayal or resentment. You don't feel worthy of expressing your emotions, especially to the person whom you felt was responsible for how you currently feel. You are very critical of yourself. You do not take time to nurture yourself. You often suffer from dehydration. You are dwelling in negative emotions so the body has become stagnant, rigid or toxic. You are from a family where you had to accept whatever was given to you. Your emotional needs were met by unpredictable moods, instability or negative reactions. This resulted in a great deal of tension and stress. You now think twice before expressing any needs.

Umbilical Hernia

See Birth – Umbilical cord, Hernia – Umbilical Hernia

Uremia

See Bleeding, Blood Problems, Fatigue, Hypertension, Kidney Problems

Emotions

You are holding onto negative emotions as it is serving you in one way or another. Your emotions have piled up. Anger and resentment that you projected and felt towards others is now being projected towards you. You are poisoning yourself with your own trauma, anger or rigidity. You have learned how to feel comfortable feeling uncomfortable in your life. You may have a fear that if you let go of how you feel then you will lose the coping and survival skills. You have learned how to survive in hostile circumstances. You have felt strong emotions for a long period of time. As a result, you started to identify with your hardships and trauma. You feel unable to communicate your resentment toward others. This will only result in judgment or criticism. You feel that no one understands you or how you feel.

Urethritis

See Bladder Problems, Inflammation / Infection, Pregnancy

Emotions

You feel intimated, irritated or angry toward your intimate partner, friends or family who triggered unresolved issues you had with a parent(s). You felt threatened and disempowered by influential people who made you believe that you are in the way. You were to be seen and not heard. You feel shame and disgust when you express your sexuality. This is often a result of being exposed to sex in a way that created negative associations. You feel anger toward an influential person that made you feel worthless.

Urinary Incontinence

See Bladder Problems, Bladder Cancer, Incontinence

Uterine Fibroid

See Female Problems, Fibroids, Polyps, Tumor, Urethritis

Emotions

You have a fear of losing your power and independence when in a relationship. Being with a man and having children might challenge your freedom and individuality. You want to break away from an old-school belief that women have to be housewives; they have to take care of everything and be a mother, role model or caretaker for everyone. You may feel resistant and unsafe to be with a man or challenged by the idea of having children. You could have a fear of the opposite sex that impacts your desire to have a relationship. This may be a pattern related to trauma from the ancestry line. This could include women who were abused and mistreated by men, during a more repressed time in history.

Uterus Problems

See Abortion, Birth, Bleeding, Eclampsia, Endometriosis, Estrogen Problems, Fallopian Tube Problems, Female Problems, Fibroids, Hysterectomy, Ovary Problems, Polyps, Pregnancy, Prolapsed Problems – Uterus

Emotions

Your inner strength and power may have been suppressed and challenged by influential people. Influential people may have felt that you represented a threat. These people may have deliberately punished and challenged your strengths, boundaries and patience. The uterus is also strongly related to a person's relationship with herself. You might feel that you are not allowed to explore your life, your creativity or sexuality and femininity. You may have been manipulated and controlled by means of shame and guilt. You experienced a challenging relationship with an influential female figure, a mother, teacher or sister.

Vaginal Thrush

See Candida – Thrush in vagina, Fungus, Vaginitis

Vaginitis

See Bacteria, Candida, Female Problems, Inflammation

Emotions

You feel angry and resentful. Your current patterns, habits or old resentments are no longer serving you. You have been holding on to anger and sexual guilt that may be triggered by your current relationships and circumstances. In the past, the anger has kept you safe and helped you to express boundaries. Now, you have moved into a new phase in your life where this habit will only sabotage new opportunities. You may feel a great deal of regret over past relationships that didn't work out. You may feel a great deal of sexual anger, as your needs are not being met in a fulfilling way. This may be tied in with feeling guilty for having sexual needs, for they are in conflict with the values that were projected at you during childhood.

Varicose Veins

See Blood Pressure, Circulatory Problems, Inflammation, Muscle Problems, Restless Leg Syndrome, Skin Problems, Ulcers, Varicose Veins

Emotions

You often have difficulty receiving support as receiving support may ultimately help you to move forward in life, whether it's a personal move or a career move. You are afraid to move forward because you don't like making changes. You sabotage receiving support as a result of this fear. You experienced a great amount of sadness in your life and missed opportunities as a result of this fear of moving forward. You know what you are worth and capable of.

Vasculitis

See Blood Problems, Heart Problems, Immune System, Inflammation, Circulation Problems, Thrombosis, Varicose Veins, Vein Problems

Emotions

You seem to feel that your truth has been manipulated by influential people's own values and beliefs. You have experienced a "hardening of the attitude" as an unconscious effort to emotionally protect yourself from others. You are simmering with anger as a result of love that has been denied. You felt deprived of many privileges during childhood. You feel there is a lack of love, support, encouragement and protection in your life. You are resentful, as you couldn't have what you wanted in relationships. You feel punished, as if you were treated unfairly.

Vein Problems

See Blood Pressure, Cardio-Vascular Problems, Circulatory Problems, Heart Problems, Inflammation, Muscle Problems, Restless Leg Syndrome, Skin Problems, Ulcers, Varicose Veins

Emotions

Love and affection were not easily expressed in the family. When influential people expressed love, it was shown and expressed in a rigid or conditional way. This has caused you to feel blocked, confused and angry. What you attract in the love department is not what you were searching for. You seem to be attracting people that are mirroring the influential people's responses and behavior toward you during childhood. The people you attract also express and show love in a controlling or rigid way. Love made you feel unsafe, as you had to provoke others in order to get a response. Love = fights, arguments, hostility, control and ultimately feeling trapped. You want to move away from these patterns, yet you know no other way of life. You fear that any new changes might cause even more ripple waves in your life. You would rather compromise your needs than rock the boat in your family life. You may also have been the scapegoat and were often wrongfully blamed.

Vertigo

See Dizziness, Eye Problems, Meniere's Disease, Tinnitus

Emotions

You often have many self-sabotaging blocks in your life. You seem to feel that you do not deserve to have things come easily to you. Any past attempts at becoming successful have been sabotaged by influential people's own self-destructive behavior. You may have been raised in a family where you felt unsafe and stuck in a fight or flight instinct. Perhaps you were exposed to volatile, unpredictable moods. You fix and adjust things constantly in an effort to avoid how you feel. You have been exposed to many unstable and unpredictable circumstances. As a result, you do not always know what to do. This pattern has overlapped into your adult life, causing a great deal of anxiety, confusion, stress or loneliness. You know how to survive within chaotic situations but have reached a point where you have lost complete control of how you feel.

Vestibular Schwannoma

See Acoustic Neuroma, Cyst, Tumor

Virus

See Cirrhosis, Herpes, Human Papillomavirus (HPV), Parasites

Emotions

Viral issues are related circumstances where people are battling out their worthiness issues. You feel that you have been deprived of many emotional needs during your childhood. You seem to feel that you had to cope with very little support, love or protection. You felt smothered by a partner that was emotionally needy or possessive. You may also have felt smothered by means of control, dominance or threats that were projected at you. You often felt that you had to fight for what you wanted, including having any needs met.

Vitiligo

See Auto Immune System, Chloasma, Immune System Compromised, Inflammation, Skin Problems

Emotions

There seems to be a great deal of ancestral trauma that has surfaced in your life. You have experienced trauma and circumstances that mirror the same emotional intensity that an ancestor experienced in their lives. There has been an accumulation of a specific kind of trauma (often feeling threatened, in danger, needing to hide and not able to control their territory). As a result, you may feel very sensitive to your environment.

Vomiting

See Nausea – Vomiting

Warts

See Skin Problems, Virus

Emotions

You feel unsure about how to proceed with a specific relationship or direction in your life. You may have experienced a stressful and tense relationship with a parent or influential person who challenged your decisions. You are very stubborn and inflexible. You have a fear of what the family might think if you moved away from the family values. You have been made to feel deeply ashamed for believing in your own values and beliefs, which is separate to your family's value system. As a result, you feel stuck in a fight or flight instinct, which has been very taxing on the immune system and your overall wellbeing.

Discussed in Volume 1: Plantar Warts (warts under feet).

Weight Problems

See Addictions – Food, Anorexia, Bulimia, Depression, Dumping Syndrome, Hyper-Somnia, Thyroid Problems, Toxins

Emotions

This could be a result of an underactive thyroid. An underactive thyroid is related to carrying a great deal of emotional baggage. You feel a great need to protect yourself from experiencing any further emotional pain. You have already had a fair share of stress, tension and rejection. You believe that you have too many shortcomings in life and no matter how much you try; you will always fail. You seem to feel that you will never have enough of what you need and you are surrounded by deprivation. You feel like a victim of circumstance whenever you are challenged. You hide and become invisible instead of standing your ground. You felt too helpless in your childhood to change the circumstances. The pattern of helplessness has now overlapped into your adult life. You are trying to compensate for the part of you that is unattractive and not perfect. Your friendliness is often a symptom of a hidden submissive nature. If you don't give in to others, you fear being rejected. Everyone needed you, yet no one offered support. This only reinforced the illusion that you have a lack of everything in your life.

Whiplash

See Accident, Back Problems, Concussion, Muscle Problems, Neck Pain, Pain, Tendon problems

Emotions

All of your rigidity has been triggered by this incident. You are holding on to rigid thoughts and patterns that no longer serve you. You seem to have a fear of moving forward without the baggage or old memories of influential people that may have caused you harm.

Whooping Cough

See Cough – Whooping Cough

Wilsons Syndrome

See Cirrhosis, Nerve Problems, Psychosis, Schizophrenia

Emotions

You feel challenged when faced with a situation that involved giving and receiving love. Love may have been expressed in a rigid, stubborn and hostile way. You are holding on to old pain, stress and tension in your life. You are sabotaging your goals. This may be the result of being belittled or undermined during childhood. You may have been part of a family that suppressed a great deal of anger, only allowing it to surface unexpectedly.

Worms

See Diarrhea, Nausea, Nerve Problems, Parasites, Rashes, Skin Problems

Emotions

You feel outside of your comfort zone and poor personal boundaries have invited parasites and possibly parasitic people into your life. You feel unworthy of asking for what you need, as your experience has taught you that you should be ashamed for expressing needs. You feel invaded by the needs and agendas of others. You do not feel worthy of expressing your own boundaries.

Wrist Problems

See Arthritis, Bone Problems (Broken), Carpal Tunnel Syndrome, Cumulative Trauma Disorder, Inflammation, Osteoarthritis, Muscle Problems, Rheumatoid Arthritis, Tendonitis, Tendon Problems

Emotions

You know what you want however, you lack the flexibility to make necessary changes to successfully create and develop what you want. You have a need to be creative with your life again. You want to follow your own journey and not someone else's agenda.

Yaws discussed in Volume 1.

See Bacteria, Bone Problems, Skin Problems, Syphilis, Warts

Yeast

See Allergies - Yeast

Yellow Fever

See Fever, Jaundice, Malaria, Nausea

Emotions

You feel frustrated and stuck. You seem to feel that you cannot change circumstances that are heading your way. You are trying to let go of how you felt in the past. You feel familiar with the trauma and stressful circumstances. The trauma seems to be the only thing that makes sense in your life at the moment. You want to rid yourself of what you do not need anymore. This could include relationships, partnerships and friendships.

Yolk Sac Tumor

See Cancer, Gonad Problems, Tumor

Emotions

Your mother may have felt suppressed, controlled or dominated by her partner while pregnant with you. Her boundaries were invaded, controlled and manipulated to suit her partner or her family's needs and demands. You seem to feel a great deal of anger that has been suppressed in your mother and may have been triggered by your personal relationships and environment. Your mother's anger is a result of not exercising her own power or expressing her needs and feeling disempowered by a partner or by influential people.

Glossary – explanation of terms

You may come across these terms in this book.

Abuse, in its broadest definition, is any crossing of a person's boundaries. Abuse generally involves intimidation or manipulation and an intrusion into another person's space. Types of abuse include physical, sexual, emotional, financial, and spiritual abuse. A useful lesson is that a person can feel abused, even though the other person does not think they have done anything wrong. Abuse is subjective and we accept the victim's account at face value during therapy, because it is their feelings that we are healing.

Acknowledgment means accepting the truth about something. It is the opposite of suppression or resistance.

Activate – when a trauma is activated (or triggered) it means that you have accessed or awakened the memory of the trauma (what happened to you) or the survival instinct (how you survived it). When the trauma is activated, you are in a trauma state. That means that you will make decisions or communicate from a place of trauma.

Attack – this is when someone is being verbally or physically attacked. The person feels unsafe, out of control or disrespected as a result. Feeling or being attacked is not necessarily a physical trauma; it can be emotional (feeling emotionally or mentally attacked). A person's ideas, opinion, truth, beliefs or values can be attacked.

Body Mind is the part of the *Triune Brain model* that corresponds with the R-complex. It is associated with basic reptile or fish abilities of acting on survival instincts. When we respond to a threat to our safety, or act to meet our most basic needs (food, shelter, the desire to reproduce), we are applying the body mind.

Boundaries define where you end and another person (or outside world) begins. This might define physical (personal) space and also mental / emotional space. For example: someone crosses your physical boundaries when they physically touch you without permission, or when they enter your physical space (such as your home). Someone crosses your emotional or mental boundaries when they verbally abuse or psychologically torment you.

Brain Mind is the part of the *Triune Brain model* that corresponds with the neo-cortex. It is associated with advanced human thought and reasoning, including language skills. When we think things through logically and communicate our reasoning, we are applying the brain mind.

Coherence means that all of your minds or centers of consciousness become one. For example: if the head (human rational brain), heart (feelings oriented mammal brain) and gut (body mind acting on instincts) all give the same answer, they are coherent. Coherence is (and should be) our natural state. It is trauma (especially at conception and in utero) that blocks us from coherence.

To complete a trauma means to finish the process that began with a traumatic experience, so that the survival instinct reaction has returned to its normal or neutral state (not stuck on or off). At this point, there is no subjective experience of trauma or lasting symptom.

Control (being controlled) – to be or feel controlled emotionally, mentally or physically. When a person's freewill is manipulated and controlled by an influential person in an unreasonable way that causes the person stress or fear. An abuser may use dominance, threats, or forms of rejection or manipulation to control and individual.

Control (being controlling) is a lack of empathy or disregard for someone else's freewill. Often this type of behavior stems from a resolved trauma related to lack of control in one's past. Abusing power and authority or position within a family, workplace or relationship.

Ego is a person's sense of self or identity. Ego creates a *boundary*; it keeps us feeling separate from others. Note that ego is neither good nor bad. It is not the goal of therapy to have no ego (in fact, that could be quite damaging). However, a useful goal would be to balance your ego, so that you can feel special and unique, without having to be separate. This would enable you to feel good about yourself without needing to be competitive or abusive of others.

Empathy is the ability to share another person's feelings. Without empathy, it is not possible to have compassion or to take into account another person's emotions. People with no capacity for empathy are considered to be sociopaths or psychopaths.

Epigenetics is the study of how the environment affects the expression of genes. The environment (e.g. emotional and physical trauma) can switch different genes on and off. The DNA itself does not change. I believe that epigenetics explains why ancestral trauma affects our emotional and physical health.

Fear is a distressing negative sensation caused by the perception that someone or something is a threat. The key element is the external threat, which distinguishes it from anxiety, which does not require an external threat. A fear might be completely rational, whereas a *phobia* is irrational.

Gut or **Gut mind** refers to listening to your body's *instincts*. In the *Triune Brain model,* it refers to the *Body mind.*

Head brain – see *Brain mind.*

Heart Mind is the part of the *Triune Brain model* that corresponds with the *limbic system.* It is associated with mammal abilities of feelings and group dynamics (behaving as a team or community, self-sacrifice to help the group). When we connect with our feelings and especially when we make decisions based on feelings, we are applying the heart mind.

Hidden benefit is a broad term, which means an internal or external benefit that we get from holding on to something, whether it is an association, trauma, symptom or something else. The term "hidden" suggests that the benefit is unconscious. Becoming consciously aware of the benefit helps to heal it, but does not always do so. Psychologists call the external benefit of a symptom secondary gain. We use the term "hidden benefit" when we are speaking more broadly about benefits that lie outside the definition of secondary gain.

An Instinct is an automatic behavior that does not require cognition or consciousness in order to occur. A learned response is not an instinct.

Key Developmental Events are key moments in the process of life, from conception through to birth. Examples include fertilization and implantation. Trauma at these moments in time can have a significant effect on our development. This suggests that instead of trying to clear any and all trauma, we can and should focus on specific traumas at those moments when we are most susceptible.

Personal responsibility means taking *responsibility* for your actions, accepting the consequences that come from those actions and understanding that what you do impacts those around you. You have a personal responsibility to take care of yourself, for example, by keeping healthy, managing your emotions, setting personal *boundaries*, and treating yourself with respect, etc. The opposite of personal responsibility might be called a "blame mentality." People with a blame mentality will always look for someone to be responsible for everything that goes wrong in their life, rather than looking within. They don't see how they might have caused the problem or how they can change things.

A Phobia occurs when a fear becomes irrational. For example: a fear of heights is a survival instinct to stop you peering off the edge of the cliff. However, if the fear prevents you from crossing bridges or boarding an aircraft, it has become a phobia. In practice, the difference between fear and phobia is not important.

Placebo is a substance that has no therapeutic effect. For example: a sugar pill is often used as a control in testing new drugs. Many people given the placebo treatment will heal; this is called the **placebo effect**. In relation to *talking therapies*, or *spiritual healing*, a placebo may be the interest that the practitioner shows in the client. Patients will often report at least a short-term benefit from any therapy, even one with no therapeutic effect.

Responsibility means being accountable for something or acknowledging that you are the cause or source of something. For example: if you take responsibility for your own life, it means that you acknowledge all the choices you have made that got you to where you are today. The opposite would be blame – if you tend to blame others for where you are in life, you aren't taking responsibility. People often take too little or too much responsibility, depending on their nature. Too much responsibility is where you feel accountable for everyone around you, such as the health and success of your friends and family. If you take too little responsibility, you might be expecting others to support you rather than being accountable for your own success.

Secondary Gain is an external benefit (usually unconscious) that a client gets from their *symptoms*. Examples include avoiding responsibility or gaining financial advantage. We can gain external benefit from many things, so not all benefits are secondary gains. For this reason, we also use the broader term *hidden benefits*.

Self-sabotage occurs when you hinder your own progress or success, usually unconsciously. Self-sabotage is usually caused by fear. This is most often a fear of success. For example: a person with a fear of being hurt in a relationship may be going on many dates but constantly sabotage them, perhaps by being late, being rude, constantly finding fault with the partner, etc. This behavior enables the client to avoid ever being in a committed relationship, which could result in being hurt. The method for clearing self-sabotage using IBS is to identify either (a) the underlying fear, which the sabotage is avoiding (success at something); or (b) the secondary gain of the self-sabotage – how is the sabotage keeping the client safe. In most cases, these two approaches will yield the same underlying cause. In some cases, it may be necessary to take both approaches.

Spiritual healing is a broad label for any of a wide variety of healing techniques (or "modalities") which require either (a) a spiritual belief in a higher power; or (b) a belief in invisible "subtle" energies. Examples include prayer healing, angel healing, Reiki, Qigong, acupuncture and chakra balancing. I don't consider IBS to be a form of spiritual healing because the effectiveness of the technique requires no belief in any spiritual causes or explanations.

Survival instincts are hard-wired *instincts* that keep us alive. The best known is the fight-or-flight response. Other instincts include the freeze response and hiding. A useful test as to whether a feeling or instinct is a survival instinct is to ask, "How many steps is this removed from my survival?" For example, fighting, fleeing or freezing can each lead immediately to your survival. By contrast, people offer "aloneness" as an instinct, and whilst it may be safer to be alone, it does not lead immediately to survival. It is too many steps removed, so it is not a survival instinct.

Sympathy is a mixture of *empathy* (the ability to feel what others are feeling) together with a desire to see change or to help the other person. You may have empathy for all people but are more likely to sympathize with close friends and family. It is sometimes said that empathy helps you to recognize people's problems but sympathy draws you into their problems. This is a reason why *therapists* must have strong professional *boundaries*.

A symptom is a physical or emotional feature noticed by a client that indicates an abnormality. A physical symptom may be an ache or pain, whereas an emotional symptom may be a strong emotion like grief or anger.

A State is the present condition or consciousness of a person at a given point in time. You could describe someone's mental state, physical state or emotional state at any moment. Their *State* includes the content and coherence of their minds.

Therapy or Therapist, when used in this course, relates to any *talking therapy* or the person who applies them. Note that different states have different rules about the word "therapy" or "therapist." You must not advertise a therapy or describe yourself as a therapist unless you hold the licenses required in your state.

Trauma is an injury or harm, which occurs when a person experiences a threat to his or her own, or someone else's safety. Examples might include physical assault, an accident, injury, or other event, which involved a threat to survival, or feeling unsafe. [This is from the technical definition from DSM-IV, pp. 424-28.] Simply witnessing harm to someone else (even remotely by photo or video) can also constitute trauma. An example might be the trauma of watching the events of September 11 2001; this caused higher stress levels in many people and their children who were in utero at the time.

A Trauma State is a *state* in which a person's trauma is *activated*. The person is responding from their trauma and survival instincts rather than a place of clarity. Generally a *trauma state* is temporary. Even if the trauma is not healed, people naturally create a level of *bypass* so that they can get on with their lives – at least until the next time the trauma is activated. Thus, most people spend their lives moving from trauma state to bypass state to trauma state.

Triggered – see Activated.

Triune Brain model is a model of the evolution of the vertebrate forebrain and behavior proposed by the American physician and neuroscientist Paul D. MacLean.

References

The body is the barometer of the soul, 1994 Annette Noontil

Your body is telling you love yourself, 2001 Lise Bourbeau

The Body Bears the Burden, Trauma, Disassociation and Disease, 2001 Robert C. Scaer, MD

Recall Healing Pyramid of Health, 2011 Gilbert Renaud

Grant McFetridge (et al), *Peak States of Consciousness: Theory and Applications*, volume 1 (2004) and volume 2 (2009)

Wikipedia, "List of diseases" Online [Available]
    http: / / en.wikipedia.org / wiki / Lists_of_diseases

Science Daily, "Babies Show Ripple Effects of Mothers Stress From 9 / 11 Trauma" Online [Available]
    http: / / www.sciencedaily.com / releases / 2005 / 05 / 050503153904.htm May, 3, 2005

Science Daily, "Mirror, Mirror In The Brain: Mirror Neurons" Online [Available]
    http: / / www.sciencedaily.com / releases / 2007 / 11 / 071106123725.htm 7 November 2007

About The Author

Evette Rose is an Author, Life Coach, Founder of Inner Beauty States (IBS). Evette was born in South Africa and grew up in Namibia, West Africa. She moved to Australia for work. She is best known for her work in helping people to resolve trauma from their past and freeing them to live successful and fulfilling lives. Evette's work is drawn from her own personal experience of moving from a difficult past into a well-balanced life and career. Evette's philosophy is that we, as a human race, are not destined to live our lives in pain due to past trauma or abuse. Humans often suppress their ability to complete or heal trauma naturally. In today's society we often suppress our pain in order to keep up with life and avoid being left behind. Fortunately, through gentle therapy, this natural internal healing instinct can be restored. Writing her books has helped Evette reach out to other people who are in need of love, support, and someone to relate to. She shares her experiences with the world in hopes that it will help people heal and provide encouragement and reassurance when they need it most. Evette is also the author of *Finding Your Own Voice* and a new title that will be out soon, *Inner Beauty States*. Evette now travels the world teaching personal development seminars.

Would you like to learn and see more? Then please visit:

www.evetterose.com

5143605R00097

Printed in Great Britain
by Amazon.co.uk, Ltd.,
Marston Gate.